IMPRESSIONS

OF

LONDON SOCIAL LIFE.

IMPRESSIONS

OF

LONDON SOCIAL LIFE

WITH OTHER PAPERS

SUGGESTED BY AN ENGLISH RESIDENCE.

BY

E. S. NADAL.

NEW YORK:
SCRIBNER, ARMSTRONG & CO.
1875.

JOHN F. TROW & SON,
PRINTERS AND BOOKBINDERS,
205–213 *East 12th St.*,
NEW YORK.

TO THAT CHIVALROUS GENTLEMAN AND HONEST FRIEND,

JUDGE JOHN P. O'SULLIVAN,

I beg to Inscribe this little Book,

WITH THE ASSURANCE THAT IN WHATEVER PART OF THE EARTH HIS FEET NOW STRAY OR TARRY, HE BEARS WITH HIM THE WARM RECOLLECTIONS OF THE AUTHOR.

PREFACE.

THIS volume of Essays records the impressions received during a residence in London, where the Author was for some eighteen months a secretary of legation. It also describes things here as they appear to one who returns to this country after a stay in England. A number of these papers have already been printed in American periodicals.

NEW YORK: *January*, 1875.

CONTENTS.

Some Impressions of London Social Life.

I WISH to record some impressions of London social life, and of that particular phase of it we call society. I may dwell upon some faults which, I should explain, are shared by society in all times and places — indeed, are quite inseparable from it, while others to be described are the peculiarities not so much of the country as of the age. Whatever be the defects and drawbacks of society, scholars and thinkers would wish to establish something like it, did they not see that, in many respects, that already established was unfit for their uses. Were it possible, they would want some common ground where men and women might meet to talk and see and be seen. What they, with their very high intentions, would desire, the rest of us would find enjoyable. When the gods had brought man into existence, they were still puzzled by the formidable problem of how he was to be amused. It was supposed that something more extended and complex than the original race would be required for that purpose; and numerous plans were submitted to the council of the gods, and were one by one rejected. At length one Olympian inventor arose and suggested that the members of the new race should find their amusement in looking at each other. This novel and audacious suggestion, though at first received with merriment and wonder, was finally adopted, and on trial was discovered to work admirably. It has certainly since proved itself to be the completest of all inventions, at once the most perfect and the simplest and most labour-saving.

I have often wondered if something like the Athenian Agora could not be devised. One of the great features of Athens, I fancy, was the active intellectual interest the people took in their society as a spectacle. The liveliest curiosity everywhere pervaded the community, and the stimulus of a public place of resort must have been great. Hither came men of all ranks and professions—merchants, poets, soldiers, sophists, and statesmen. When Socrates or Cleon passed, every pedlar had his jibe and every huckster his bit of scandal. The whole market-place was full of mirth, movement, gaiety, gossip, and curiosity. There is, at least, one modern institution which has some points of similarity to the Agora: I mean London society. The resemblance is one more of form than of character. It is like it in the fact that it brings numbers of people into association, or rather contiguity, and that in it we see constantly all the noted people of the day. Here the likeness ends: the life and variety are not there.

Yet, easy as it is to find fault with, London society is far the most perfect thing of the kind in the world, and it must be a dull man who would fail to extract amusement and pleasure from it. Were it a little less hard and rude, and were there a little more liberty for individualities, one might spend a lifetime in it with profit. As a spectacle, it is valuable for its profuseness, its pomp of life, the beautiful women and famous men we see. There is, moreover, something of moral education in it. We get a certain strength —of a kind, indeed, which we should not take long to acquire, and, having acquired, should not take a lifetime to practise, but still a kind of strength—silent resistance, and ease in the presence of people who are indifferent and critical. The dowagers are the persons in conversing with whom one experiences the greatest growth of character. Some large and listless mother, whose eyes are following the fortunes of her charges over the field, and who has asked you for the fourth time the question you have already answered for the third—to go on discoursing to such a person as calmly and fluently as Cato does to the universe is a great and difficult thing. There is not a pleasure in it, nor indeed a rapture, but there is real growth and building up in a certain amount of it.

But the moral education of society is scarcely its

most important service. There is a large class of men to whom success in it is the main object of life. To them it furnishes a profession, and one in which they are sure in time to succeed. He who in the bloom of youth is bidden to dance at some great lady's ball is sure, with average luck and persistence, to go to breakfast in his toupee. It gives the swell something to live for. When he has attained the Marquis of This, the Duke of That shines yet ahead of him. The way is plain, and there is no limit to the possibilities of its extension. From round to round of the Jacob's ladder of fashion the aspiring climber may ascend indefinitely. There is always something a little ahead. To tread all the ways of Mayfair, to sound all the depths and shoals of Belgravia, were indeed a hopeless task. But it has many sorts of uses for many sorts of people. Mothers there exhibit their marriageable wares. Politicians put their heads together. The Earl of Barchester asks a Cabinet minister to appoint a friend. But the old gentlemen who go to look on and take their daughters get the most out of it. It is especially pleasant for them by contrast with the treatment they receive in this country. Here the fathers of families creep about among their daughters' suitors in a very abject and humble manner. "What talk is there of fathers when there is such a man as Orlando?" The old men in England are much more defiant and unmanageable. They do not strike their flags to the young ones, as is their habit with us. They confront age with fine clothes, the locks right from the hand of the hair-dresser, and the air of success and authority. The condition of an Englishman who has grown grey in honours, who has a star and a decoration and the health and vanity to wear them properly, is by no means an unhappy one. (Decorations should be given to suit complexions; kings and colleges should award blue ribbons to blond men and red ribbons to dark men.) If, besides his fortunate accidents, he has humour, sensibility, and an individuality, his is really an enviable lot. In the most rigid of societies, wealth, rank, and success clear a way for individuality. They make one elbow-room. An eccentric clerk in the Admiralty would very soon find himself on the curbstone; the eccentric nobleman, on the contrary, is a popular personage, and has a recognised position in all the novels. Even hard and supercilious people are not apt to question the wit and manners of one whom kings and learned societies have indorsed. A stare need not make him check his humour. He may be a strong and a natural person, if he chooses. It used to delight me to watch one old man who had run a career in literature and politics, and to whom the world had given all its good things. He protected himself with the best of Poole's tailoring. He wore a decoration which suited his complexion perfectly. He was none of your cravens. He met old age with hand gaily extended in the jauntiest, boldest way in the world. With a bearing humorously perverse and imperious, with a pair of yellow-grey eyes flashing over his eagle beak, he moved through the throng; shaking hands pleasantly with many, complimenting the mammas, and hectoring the maidens, whose conversation he corrected with mock severity, and whom he cautioned against slang. Such of the young ladies as received his reproof demurely, he looked down on with approbation; while those who were saucy pleased quite as well, as they gave him opportunity for more extended reprimand. If age ever retains the vanity, humour, and kindness of youth, this old man must have had a pleasant time. The only drawback is, that the people who to-night are flattered by his smile may, a week hence, be reading his obituary with that contempt we instinctively feel for a man who has just ceased to live. The death of a successful man of the world affects our way of thinking of him much as any other reverse in his affairs—the loss of his fortune, for instance, or the favour of his party. We cannot help reflecting that he must now take in a little sail, that he must in future abate a little his demand upon society.

But for the average man the very last thing society does is to give him an opportunity to express himself. Self-suppression is the lesson it inculcates by precept and by very strong example. The man of society must imitate the patience of the processes of nature. He must act as though he intended to go out for ever, and was in no hurry to get the good of it. No wise man attempts to hurry London society. The people who compose it never hurry. But if the man of society be unselfish and be careful to retain his sanity, its chief good is in what it offers him to look at—the carriages flashing back and forth at the dinner-hour, looking like caskets or Christmas-boxes with the most wonderful lining and furniture (the drapery and lace almost floating out of the windows), the balls and parties, the acres of fair-armed British maidens through which he may wander as in a wilderness, the odours of the midnight gardens, the breath of the dawn, and the first flush of sunrise over Hyde Park as the drowsy cabman wheels him homeward and to bed. Every spring he may watch for the reappearance of some queen of the last season, as for the coming of the flowers. To a mind capable of pleasure it must often be a joyous and delightful spectacle, and always an amusing one. But if a man be subject to feelings of pique and envy, and allow fortunes better than his own to make him wretched, there could hardly be a worse place for him. I knew one man, foolish fellow! who, instead of giving himself up to the admiration of the ladies, and the graces and peculiarities of the dancers, had held aloof and had been unhappy because people took so little notice of him. He told me that, when he saw other men successful and smiled upon, he used to stand back and try to look "devilish deserving." "Wisdom and worth were all he had." "I have since found out," he remarked, "what a very poor expedient it was. For success in society, either here or anywhere else, I had as lief be accused of forgery as of modest merit."

I found everywhere an excessive respect of the individual for the sentiment of the mass—I mean in regard to behaviour. In matters of opinion there is greater latitude than with us. Nowadays a man in England may believe anything he chooses; the reason being, I suppose, that beliefs have not much root or practical importance. Authority seems to have left the domain of thought and literature, and to have invaded that of manners. Of the two sorts of tyranny, I think I should prefer the first. I should rather be compelled to write my poetry in pentameters, and to speak with respect of the Church and the Government, than to be forever made to behave as other people dictate. I know Englishmen do not accept this as true of themselves. One of them, to whom I had hinted something of the sort, said, "Oh, I don't know; we do about as we please." Precisely; but they have lived so constantly in the eyes of other people, have got so used to conforming, that they never think of wanting to do what society would disapprove of. They have been so in the habit of subduing whatever native individuality they possess, that they have at last got rid of it. Of course, it would be impossible to make them believe this. They mistake their inattention, the hostile front they present to the world, and their indifference to the strictures of foreigners when they are abroad, for real independence and a self-reliant adherence to nature. But there seems to me to be something conventional even about the rude and lounging manners of which they are so proud. It is like the "stand-at-ease" of soldiers. It would be highly improper and contrary to orders to do anything else.

Englishmen appeared to me to be criticising themselves away. It is not only among Englishmen of fashion, nor solely in England, that this is the case. The age everywhere partakes of it. It has come to attach great importance to proper externals, to seemliness, to a dignified and harmonious behaviour. What unexceptionable people in their private lives are the writers of the day! Artists used to be envious and backbiting: if they retain such feelings at present, they are certainly not candid. It cannot be that the world has made such progress in a few years as to have quite got rid of the passions of spite and envy. We fear the age has caught cold and the disease has been driven in. Certainly we have come to devote an exceedingly particular and microscopic care to externals; we give such attention to our walk and conversation, we are so careful to avoid faults and littlenesses of demeanour, that we seem to have acquired some sort of negative Puritanism or Pharisaism. This is true of ourselves, and it is true of all educated English people; but the disease reaches its extremest form among Englishmen of fashion and quality. I once asked one of the kindest and cleverest of them I knew, "Can a young man in this country read poetry to the ladies—not his own, of course, but out of a book?" "No," said he, "that would be rather com-pro-mis-ing" (shaking his head and pronouncing the word slowly). On reflection, I did not remember having done that thing myself for some years, but I hardly had it classified as one of the things not to be done under any circumstances.

In this very great self-consciousness and doubt as to what to say and do, it was an advantage to have some particular tone set and the range of conversation narrowed within some well-understood limits. By this, language, as a medium of expression, is abolished, and becomes a means of getting along comfortably with friends. Certain things are set apart as good for men to converse upon—the races, horse-flesh, politics, anything in short, providing it is not discussed in a definite or original manner.

No man should say anything which might not be very well said by any one else. Each man has an infallible guide in the rest. He must set his clock by them, and regulate it carefully when it inclines to go faster. The following is a simple and easily-understood specimen of a club conversation :—

First Speaker. "Are you going to Aldershot to-morrow?"

Second Speaker. "No."

Here follows a pause of several minutes.

First Speaker. "Why aren't you going to Aldershot to-morrow?"

Second Speaker. "O, I hate Aldershot."

Here follows a pause of longer duration, during which the first speaker reads over the *Pall Mall Gazette* for the third time.

Second Speaker. "Waiter, bring me gin and seltzer."

This one might call the unit of a club conversation, upon which more elaborate remark may be superadded at will.

We are of course always bound to pitch our voices to the ears of those around us. As a rule, we must expect people to talk about trivial matters; it would be a great bore if they did otherwise. But now and then we need not be surprised at a little genuine laughter or a hearty greeting between friends. But in the clubs, from what I saw, there rarely seemed to be any abandon or heartiness. There was roseate youth with the finest health, with beauty, with a flower in the button-hole, with horses to ride in the Row, with fine raiment and sumptuous living every day, with the smiles of mammas and the shy adoration of the maidens. Yet I have seen old men who seemed far more happily self-forgetful and with more enthusiasm for enjoyment. The young men have deteriorated from the energy of their fathers of forty years ago, who must have been a very amusing class of men. The strong pressure of public sentiment prevents these young men from acquiring the old physical vigour and freedom of the British upper class; and as they have no task set them they are driven unavoidably into dulness. They never swear, or rarely. The "demmes" and "egads" of their ancestors are quite out of employment. They even sin with a certain decorum. For instance, it is very "bad form" to dance with the ladies at the casinos, though there is no impropriety in leaving those places in their company. The few men who are literary and intellectual make, perhaps, the weakest impression. The thin wash of opinion which forms their conversation evaporates, and leaves a very slight sediment. They have that contagious weariness I have noticed in the agricultural population along the water-courses of Illinois and Missouri. In the latter it is the result of fever and ague, and the long eating of half-baked bread. The voices of those people seemed to struggle up from a region below their lungs, and in them the peculiarity, besides wearying, intensely repelled and disgusted. In men as charmingly dressed and beautifully clean as these Englishmen, the offensive quality was missed, but there was the same weariness and a vapidity that inoculated and subdued you. There often seemed to me an effeminate sound in the talk, not only of the intellectual sort, but even of the faster men. Should the ghosts of their uproarious ancestors ever rustle through those halls of Pall Mall and St. James's Street, they must marvel, I fancy, to see the young bloods of the present sitting about and comparing experiences of vaccination with the minuteness of old ladies at a religious tea-party.

It is an old folly, it may be said, that of decrying the present, and I may be reminded that most men are human, no matter what the age or the country in which they live. There is truth in that; but we may easily see how very different men may be whom centuries divide, when we consider that most important fact of the human mind—mood. How diverse are the thoughts and passions which rule the fast following movements of a single human life! How diverse the lives of individual men! How widely separate from our own may be the feelings of men between whom and ourselves many years intervene, and of whom no living soul remains to speak. There was a day when people were less suspicious of each other than nowadays, when they were freer and far brighter. Talk like that of which we read in Boswell's "Life of

Johnson," "The Vicar of Wakefield," and the "Selwyn Correspondence" is not heard now. I have noticed the fluency of some very charming old ladies. They address you with an unhesitating talkativeness, which is not of this time. They have never asked themselves, "How did I appear when I said this?" or "Was not that gesture or that expression of countenance peculiar?" It would seem, then, that the monologue which is so characteristic of the novel of fifty years ago was no invention of the novelist, but that people really talked in that way. They did not skirmish behind wary short sentences as do the lovers in Mr. Trollope's books. Why, if you proposed to one of the young ladies of that period, she replied in a speech covering full a page and a half of Miss Edgeworth, perfectly fluent and grammatical, every word of which could be parsed from beginning to end. If she rejected you, the discourse was sure to contain many and most irreproachable moral sentiments. Yet those very young ladies upon occasions could very nearly swear. On the decorous pages of Miss Austin we find expressions which nowadays would be considered wicked. The proper and satirical Emma, and the very charming Elizabeth, say "Good God!" "My God!" Exquisite profanity! It would have wheedled the heart out of a travelling colporteur with a bundle of tracts. Ah, fresh blooming maidens with the blue waving plumes, what joy it would have been to have met you, and to have heard from your own lips those shocking expressions some blissful morning long ago, on a breezy hill-top, and near the foliage of a rustling oak!

The complete banishment of profanity from the conversation of men of fashion seemed to me a curious phenomenon. I do not believe it could have been accomplished in any country where example had less authority. The common modern oaths you hear very little; as to the archaic and Homeric forms, they have quite gone out. I never met a man, however aged, who used those expressions. I used constantly to see one old gentleman who always came arrayed in the traditional blue coat and brass buttons, buff waistcoat, and great neckcloth of the Regency. I fancied he might be like that

South American parrot of which Humboldt tells, that was the sole remaining creature to speak the language of a lost tribe. I never had the pleasure, however, of hearing him express himself. He silently surveyed the moving throng. The present, perhaps, seemed dull to him. He had heard, a fine May morning long ago, in Piccadilly, the horn of the coachman ringing up the street, and had awaited the stopping of the coach at Hatchett's, to see such blooming faces looking merrily out of the windows, and the ladies in the short waists and petticoats of the time alighting from the top. Somewhere away in one of those shires whose name recalls the green fields and the sound of the milk in the pail, he had kissed a country cousin under one of the big bonnets they wore when the century and he and his sweetheart were all in their teens.

In the parlours the narrow range of thought and conversation is even more noticeable than at the clubs. Here the ladies set the tone ; and kind as they usually are, bright and pretty as they often are, there is unmistakably among them an unconsciousness of all outside certain narrow limits that custom has prescribed for them. The freedom and gaiety which are not uncommon in the parlours of Americans of the best class will be hard to find in the drawing-rooms of English fashionables. They *talk*, professedly. Upon those common topics which should form the ordinary conversation they do very well, and, among the brighter of them, a kind of wit and wisdom is permitted. But that is apt to be *à la mode*. The wit is badly watered. I am not sure, however, that fashionable wisdom and watered wit are peculiar to London. All society-wit is somewhat diseased. The wit of rich and idle men is poor. It is curious that they who have nothing to do but to make jokes should make such very poor ones. There are a few recipes afloat from which most of these fine things are evidently prepared. The fashionable joke is usually accompanied by the fashionable gesture, and an expression of inward illumination which the state of the mind hardly justifies. Though as to artificial pantomime and vocal inflection, there is less of that among the English "respectables" than among our own. It may seem to contradict this, but really does not, when I say that our own fashionable manners are borrowed from the English. English people must speak in some way, and their peculiarities, as a rule, are proper and natural. Our imitative and impressible society leaders, seeing something admirable in English aristocratical style, copy the accents and gestures, forgetting that they too would seem admirable to others were they to speak naturally.

As a rule, women in English society are remarkably natural—negatively natural, I mean. English girls are particularly simple and unassuming. They are innocent of all effort to impress or astonish. As all womankind does and should do, they make themselves as pretty as they can; but as to personal superiorities, their educators do not lay enough stress upon such things to make them ambitious to excel in that way. All young ladies are taught a certain mode of deportment, which is excellent so far as it goes. The chief precept of the code, whether inculcated openly or by the silent feeling of society, is that each young lady must do as the rest. That "young English girl," who is the theme of the novelists and the magazine bards and artists, easily merits all the adulation she receives. Does not all the world know, is it not almost an impertinence to say, that for dignity, modesty, propriety, sense, and a certain soft self-possession, she has hardly her equal anywhere? But the British maiden is taught that ambition in character is not a desirable thing. The naturalness and propriety which accompany this state of mind are not particularly admirable. It is very different from that propriety which is the result of elevation of character, of conclusions intimately known and constantly practised. People who have activity and ambition are very apt to be affected, and very apt to unduly crave recognition. That we ask to be thought superior, shows at least that we prize superiority. When the young are left to their own growth, and no restrictive tariff is put upon individuality, we may expect a little nonsense. Society will certainly do a good thing for the young if it teaches them the folly of a desire for recognition. But this society does not do, I fear. It merely instructs them not to ask for recognition, because by so doing they make a bad impression. It has done them a still more doubtful service, if, in giving them this very good trait, it has also taught them to emphasise less strongly the superiorities of character and conduct.

I have said that English-society people make but little effort to impress or astonish; and I explained that they have no wish to be thought individually remarkable, because that sort of ambition among them is a very exceptional thing. What they do value is the "getting on;" and the inevitable effect of living among them is to make one think that that is the best thing one can do. Certainly those old familiar ideas of the poets and moralists, "truth, innocence, fidelity, affection, &c.," which one always felt at home with in the snug corners of the parlours at the village sewing-circles, suddenly became strange to me and very unreal and whimsical. They danced off at a distance in the oddest and most fantastical manner. If anybody sneered at "upholstery," or spoke contemptuously of rank and fashion, you at once fancied some one had snubbed him; if he praised virtue, you suspected him of wanting a dinner. But while the lust of the eyes and the pride of life are everything to upper-class Englishmen, you hear wonderfully little said about these things. Carlyle and Thackeray, the poets and satirists and the goody old maids who write the novels, though they have quite shut the mouths of these brave gentlemen, have by no means driven such thoughts out of their hearts. To give you to understand that they are persons of consequence, they would think the last degree of vulgarity. Yet, if they do not claim consequence, it is not because they do not value consequence. They know that to assert openly their demand is not the best way to have it accorded them. The avidity of Mrs. Governor Brown and Mrs. Judge Jones for the best rooms at the hotels, and the recognition and sympathy of all the railway conductors, is unknown in England. But the two manners, so different apparently, are not so different essentially. Both demand consideration and consequence—the one only more successfully than the other. The quiet demeanour, the sedulous avoidance of self-assertion, the critical look, the slightly reserved bearing, say very plainly, "See, I am a person of consequence." Both make the same inferior claim. The one makes it in a wise, refined, and successful way; the other in a foolish, vulgar, and unsuccessful way.

"Pose" is the name given to this wise, refined, and successful manner of self-assertion. It may be defined as the quality of absolute quiescence. By the aid of it we move with the semblance of unconsciousness through a throng of which we are inspecting every individual. Society has discovered (what the young find it so hard to learn) that by looking quite blank we may keep people altogether in the dark as to what we are thinking about. That which Mr. Phunky found so difficult—to look as though no one were looking at him—London society has learned to do. Yet I think that some other quality besides mere quiescence is necessary to "pose." That we will suppose to be some beauty (whether physical or spiritual) of face or form. An unconscious costermonger would not be imposing. I have seen flunkies who possessed the quality to a greater degree than their masters, and who were yet not admirable. A thing must be beautiful absolutely before it can be beautiful in any one condition—particularly in that of rest. No doubt the young men are as fine-looking a lot of fellows as can be found. They have good physiques, which they keep in good condition; they have had an education among people of breeding and cultivation; they have been at the best schools, and brought away such culture as they could not help getting; they have had respect and consideration from their cradles; they know very well they have nothing to ask of society. But besides all this, they owe most to the pains which they lavish upon their exteriors. That last is an important point. Let Carlyle deride the Stultz swallow-tail. The Stultz swallow-tail and the white waistcoats, and the gold chains, and the wonderful linen, and the silk stockings, and the beautiful boots—these between them do work wonders. The young dons at the universities and the young clergy of England—than whom no finer race of gentlemen exists, candid, catholic, modest, learned, courteous—are yet not so beautiful as the men of Pall Mall and St. James's Street. The reason is that they do not so generally seek the outdoor life, and especially that they give no such scrupulous and continuous care to the decoration of the ambrosial person.

In English ladies, "pose" is particularly admired, yet I am not sure that the novelists do not make too much of it. The female phenomenon at a circus is trained to stand with one foot on the back of a galloping horse, and yet not for a moment lose her equable expression of countenance. Surely, then, it were no such great thing to teach a lady to move amid a throng of well-disposed people with the appearance of equanimity and unconsciousness. The ladies are beautiful, especially the younger and softer of them; they choose to stand still, and the impression which is really due to some quality of face or form or spirit is ascribed to attitude. But I doubt if quiescence is the highest attainable condition of mind and body. Grace is beauty become expressive and vital. That is the quality which must delight us while we move upon the earth, and we are not content with any state of things which robs us of it. We shall not always be here, and we are impatient that whatever there is lovely in life should be in haste to express itself. Grace, I should say, was the expression of a beautiful past. It finds egress, we know, in any sort of action — walking, sewing, reading, or singing— but most of all in dancing. Here, fortunately, the baneful influence of "pose" is counteracted. The ball seems to be the invention of some good friend of humanity to force people to be quite themselves. Self-indulgence and conceit generate ugliness; virtue and self-denial beget beauty, and we know how necessary it is that people should always be expressing these things. No training of the body can eradicate vulgarity; no awkwardness or inexperience of limb can suppress grace. With what odious sensations the trained dancing-girls of the Alhambra afflict us! What indescribable pleasure some little creature's mistakes who blunders in the Lancers afford us!

"Pose" has been adopted by English people of fashion in self-defence. London and Texan societies have this one point in common—they all go armed, even to the women. As acquaintances in the South-west discuss politics over their slings and cocktails, with knives and revolvers half hidden in their belts, so the London swell, as you meet him at the club or the party, hardly conceals under his waistcoat and watch-chains the handles of his weapons of defence; and, set like jewels in the girdle that zones a lady's waist, you detect the dearest little gemmed and mounted implements of destruction. The Englishman conducts himself as though he were in an enemy's country. In the strictest apostolic sense he regards this life as a warfare. "And well he may," he would say. "Consider what people we meet, what dangers we encounter by sea and land, on the promenade, in the park, and at the watering-place. The *parvenu* walks abroad in daylight. All about us are people who don't know their grandfathers. Everywhere rich contractors and lotion-sellers lie in ambush. It behoves us to tread cautiously. And not only are we in constant dread of these people, but we must be for ever on our guard against those of our own sort. If we are affable to our superiors, they may think us familiar; if we are civil to our equals, they may fancy we think them better than ourselves. So, amid imminent perils from the insults of the great, from the snubs of equals, and the familiarities of inferiors, we move through this dangerous wilderness of society."

Of the external advantage of London society I have already spoken. Its machinery is nearly perfect. One meets numbers of persons who not only bear themselves perfectly, but seem to think and feel almost with perfection; women sensible and gracious, men from whom reflection and high purpose have removed every trace of triviality. Parties and receptions have this advantage; we have the perfection of social ease with those to whom we are under no obligation to be agreeable. The guests cannot be unconscious and oblivious of the host, nor the host of the guests. But between those who meet on common ground there may be silence or conversation, just as is most comfortable. Hence the benefit of such an organised social establishment as London possesses. The great distinction which rank and money obtain in England may perhaps be irksome to those who spend their lives in the midst of its society. To a stranger or sojourner, it is a novel and interesting feature. One felt that here was company which, however it might be in Saturn and Jupiter, no set of tellurians at least could affect to despise. You enjoyed this sensation. All round this wide planet, through the continents and the islands of the sea, among the Franks and the Arabs, the Scandinavians, the Patagonians, and the Polynesians, there were none who could give themselves airs over this. The descendants of Adam, the world over, could show nothing better.

English Sundays and London Churches.

I DOUBT if there is, upon the outside, an uglier or more unattractive holiday in the world than Sunday in an English or American town. There is something in the spectacle of the closed shops and barred windows, the long, deserted business thoroughfare, and in the ringing of the iron cellar doors over which your feet rattle drearily, to the last degree desolate and inhospitable. Even in the parks and city squares the day does not lose its disconsolate aspect. The shoemaker and his wife trundling their baby carriage afflict us with a sense of commiseration. His Sunday clothes and his wife's parasol and their solemn, circumspect walking about, suggest most vividly his unhappy, shabby toil, his unending drudgery.

Can there be anything but ugliness in a city square upon a Sunday, with an iron bench to sit upon, a gravel path to walk upon, a policeman near at hand, and the sight of three or four smart young clerks condemned to spend the day in each other's company. There is, however, in many American towns (I never saw anything of the kind in London), a street where the nice people walk up and down on Sunday afternoons. The young ladies are pretty and gay and loquacious, and the young gentlemen, though a trifle overdressed, are happy and endeavour to be agreeable. On a winter or autumn afternoon, the fine promenade of an American city is bright and splendid. There is something a little hard, something not quite warm and generous, in the spectacle of the long, cold, gay street. Yet the scene is not unpleasing. The polished window-pane is now and then lit up with a flickering ray of the firelight within. Certainly the day is not without austerity even here. But the neighbourhood of friends in a great city finds one well contented with the severity and peculiarity of the religious festival of the week. I am willing to put up with the abolition of the shop-windows, and the desolation of streets so bright on other days, with the depressing hilarities of the people, and the dismal bits of green grass, with fountains, iron benches, policemen, and baby-carriages. The tinge of gloom which hangs over the elegant quarter of the town is agreeable rather than otherwise. I am glad of the Puritan reminiscence which yet hangs about our Sunday. It is well that there should be one day in the week which we are under some vague obligation not to give to trivialities, when at times we shall even repress that laughter and joking at the sound of which dreams and emotions are apt to break away and vanish, when the lights are lowered and fingers wander over the keys, and "The spacious firmament on high," and "By cool Siloam's shady rill," are sung by the voices of the kind and good.

The English Sunday is more sombre than our own. Here the day wears more of a holiday aspect; the people in the streets look happier and are better dressed. The genteel English think it common and snobbish to dress much on Sunday. Of course they ascribe this notion to their nicer sense of propriety; but how much of it is due to superior taste and sanctity, and how much to the tradition that snobs dress on Sunday because persons of their station are compelled to work on other days, I do not pretend to decide. One may say that the English, as a rule, regard Sunday with rather more sobriety and strictness than ourselves. They think it is godless to stay away from church; and it is to the churches one must go to see the English Sunday. We, in this country, have always had a poetic curiosity and interest in the churches and parsonages of England. The "decent church" (inimitable adjective!) when, for the first time, on the road from Liverpool to London, one sees it crowning a well-clipped, humid hill-top, softly returns to the imagination as something known in infancy and forgotten. Ever since childhood our minds have been filled with innumerable stories and poems about the parsons and parsonages. There is the Vicar of Wakefield, and there is the clergyman in the "Deserted Village;" and, later, we are familiar with many admirable or amusing parsons or parsons' wives and daughters on the pages of

Miss Austin and Trollope. The clergyman seems to have been the best man in their society to unite in his person virtue and gentility with tragical poverty. On the other hand, there is in the lives of many clergymen's families just that *plenum* of earthly comfort which is alluring for the gentler uses of literature, just that happy balance of circumstances which equally removes the household from the ugliness of want, and from the pretension which is the peril of too much success. The parson has been called the "centre of English society." High and low, rich and poor, all group themselves about him, and compute their position by reference to him. He touches the community at every point; he may know everybody, though his place is a very variable and accidental one. His importance, of course other things being equal, is in proportion to his income. He is a greater man in the country than in town. Some parsons are very much greater than others. Between a bishop and a poor curate there exists what the novelists would call a "gulf." Indeed, I am told that a young curate, when speaking to a bishop in the street, would be likely to take off his hat and stand bareheaded. In London, the priest appears to lose himself amidst the crowd ; but even there he retains an intrinsic identity and distinctiveness which nobody else possesses.

We have, besides, been attracted by the artistic and poetical qualities of the Church of England. It possesses these attractions, not because it is a State Church, but because it is a National Church. It is the Church of all, and, because the people in humble and middle life outnumber the great and the fortunate, it is more the church of the poor than of the rich. This fact gives it substance and depth, and a sombre strength, like the chill sod and damp winds of their autumn evening. In the Church the people have for ages been christened, married, and buried ; indeed, any other kind of religious establishment has a look either shabby or glaringly brand-new. With us it is always the particular church, say, at the corner of Moyomensing Avenue and 18th Street, which attracts or repels one. Is it a good place to go ? Do we like the clergyman, and do we like the people ? One of the best parts of any Church Service here,

I take it, is shaking hands with acquaintances going down the aisles. We go here to those houses which attract and please, which are the brightest and happiest-looking. The minified cathedrals, where gloom was secured by the same cheap means by which one can get it in any pantry, namely, by having no windows, are replaced by houses of worship more fit and sensible. We have no old churches; and antiquity here is so weak and unimportant, that people do well in ceasing altogether to imitate its solemn and pathetic impressions. How slight and feeble is our past, the man will feel who loiters in Trinity church-yard, or strolls for an hour in St. Paul's, the interior of which wonderfully resembles an old English church. What comes to us from pre-revolutionary times is scarcely more inspiring than the rubbish left in an attic by the people who move out to those who move in. Who that drops his ticket at Wall Street Ferry cares to remember that, on that spot, George and Martha Washington landed from Virginia ninety years ago; or who of the crowds that flock hourly about the Exchange calls to mind that, on the balcony of a building which once stood there, the first president was inaugurated? The mighty To-Day of the continent is scarcely conscious of these trifles. It is different in England. George III., with his tumultuous, triumphant Empire, and his thundering Waterloos and Trafalgars, curbs the conceit and insolence of the living. So far as duration goes, America has had the very respectable past of nearly four centuries. But, whatever is ancient in point of time by association with this continent, seems to partake of its newness. What is old here does not at all become precious because it is rare. It is rather swallowed up in the all-pervading, all-forgetting present. A tomb-stone with 1790 scratched upon it is a less impressive object here than in Europe. The occupant has no constituency; there are too few of him to make it worth while to take him into account. But even the recent past in Europe is strong, because of the multitudes which disappear with a generation, and of the ages full of life and history upon which it lies. The names over the chancel of men who fell with Nelson, and the tablets upon the walls, not a half century old, appeal to us with a strange earnestness.

There is no doubt that these English temples possess sublime and fervid impressions which houses of worship of yesterday cannot produce. Yet the services in many of them, particularly in the West-End, are very dull and vapid. The churches were a third full, with pretty much everybody asleep or inattentive. The most devout and enthusiastic worship is to be found in those parts of London inhabited mainly by the lower middle classes—people who live by trades and small shops. In some churches, where the pews are reserved until the time for the service to begin, the outside public range themselves along the aisle, waiting to take the unoccupied seats when the moment comes. In other churches the pews are thrown open during the evening service, and anybody can come in and take a seat, the only precedence being such as long occupation and courtesy give. I remember a young lady who hustled me out of a comfortable corner on the plea that it was "hers." There she sat and opened her prayer-book and surrendered herself almost greedily to her ecstasy and meditation. How she valued that snug corner I could tell from the warlike expression of her countenance, when for a moment I looked sceptical of her right to eject me.

This was at St. Dominic's, with the curate of which church I had the good fortune to contract an acquaintance. The curate of St. Dominic's was a very good, laborious, and capable man. He preached two or three sermons on Sunday; his evenings were occupied with lectures and charities; during five days of the week he taught a great city school. The rest of the time he took in writing his two sermons, visiting the sick and burying the dead, in reading the Bible to all the bed-ridden old women in the parish, and in baptising certain red and blue-faced, black-haired and very tender babies. How shall I describe him—a saint without a feebleness, a humorist without scepticism, an Englishman without a trace of the egotist, a tireless worker and an unquestioning child of duty; yet with the most generous sense of enjoyment, and a most modest charity for the indolent and the semi-virtuous. I had a note to him from a friend who had met him in Switzerland. With his countenance I saw a good deal of St. Dominic's.

Often on Sunday evenings at 7 o'clock I used to call at the curate's lodgings for the chance of a walk with him to church, or rather a trot, for we were nearly always late, the parson stopping to tack a tail on to his sermon. It was a mile away, and the chimes of St. Dominic's were clanging as we brought up the vestibule. It was an ancient building, standing in what is called the "City,"—a district inclosed by the old walls and now entirely taken up by trade. I got my seat in church, and when the bell stopped, the procession of choristers, dressed in white, began to move up the aisle, the youngest and tenderest coming first, the older and taller following. The little ones were often beautiful boys, with the soft tender English complexion, and looked like angels, though I often saw them nudging each other when they were responding the loudest, and communicating by dumb show, with spelling upon their fingers and with grimaces. Their faces were so clean, and they had their hair so well brushed, that it was easy to see that some neat and proud mother had inspected every one of them. One little fellow in particular looked as if his mother had followed him all about the room, holding him by the chin, brushing his forehead and temples violently as he retreated, and, perhaps, giving him now and then a crack on the head with the hair-brush. The procession grew coarser as it grew older; the difference between the little and the big choristers was much like that between young and tender leeks and onions gone to seed. The choristers were, I suppose, taken almost entirely from the families of small shopkeepers and mechanics. Directly behind the grown choristers, and attired very much like them, came the clergy; and the contrast between their countenances showed more plainly than anything I remember seeing, the unmistakable unlikeness of gentlemen to persons who are not gentlemen. There were the well-defined, educated faces of two or three young clergymen, and in a singular contrast was the loutish, indistinct chaos in the countenances of the overgrown singers.

The curate preached always in the evenings, and led a good part of the service. His sermons were delivered in a low, musical monotone or recitative. They were thoughtful and well expressed, excellent sermons, among the best I heard in London ; but what made them especially admirable was the manifest purity of the man, the reality of his goodness. Whether he read or preached, or prayed, or sat silent, you felt the influence of a devoted spirit. It is the sort of man he is, not so much what he says, that makes a clergyman a good one. You would not care to have a vulgar, superficial, or conceited person sit in your room and occupy your attention for an hour. It is just as unpleasant to have any such man moving constantly before your eyes in church, praying, reading, and exhorting. Of vulgarity one sees very little among the English clergy, but, of course, most clergymen, like most other people, do not possess very clear ideas, and it is necessary that they be exhibiting their lack of strength during the whole time they occupy the eyes of the congregation. Their manner of reading the Bible seems to be altogether without sense or reason. They take the promises, the revelations, the ecstasies, the lamentations, and the genealogies all in the same voice, and at the same pace. I remember once to have heard, in the afternoon service at Westminster Abbey, a clergyman reading the Scriptures in a heavy, sonorous voice, with which he was obviously very well contented. Paul, in the chapter read, has been speaking in a lofty, Apostolic strain, which the agreeable baritone suited very well. But he closes the epistle with some commonplace messages, which are manifestly not to be read with the same sublimity of enunciation as the other parts of the chapter. But the clergyman grandly intoned, "Bring Zenas, the lawyer-r-r-r-r," and the cadences of this bathetic expression rolled among the arches of the cathedral and over the heads of the people. The curate of St. Dominic's intoned the service also, and with the motions of his voice his large congregation was instinctively in sympathy. His reading was affecting, as I have said, owing, not so much to any grace of manner, or agreeable vocal cadences (though his voice was a sweet one), as to the purity and devotion of his spirit. Some more modern sorts of sin, I used to think, though, might have very well found their way into his liturgy. Could he not have elided "From false doctrine, heresy and schism," and have intoned instead, "From inconstancy and vain obliviousness, from ennui, lassitude, and all self-admiration!"

St. Dominic's was one of the oldest of the city sanctuaries, its history stretching way back before Elizabeth. The church was destroyed and rebuilt at the time of the great fire. Its aisles have been the resting-place of city worthies as long as London has had Lord Mayors, or London women have been comely. Their quaint memorials were upon the windows—"Thomas Watson, citizen, of Milk Street,—1513." How many generations of listless children, lying back in these pews during the long service, have spelt out his virtues on the marble underneath, and wondered what a quaint old fellow he was, and how strange it must be to be dead so long, and have one's name scratched in such queer characters under the painted figures of saints and martyrs, then sighed to think what an age it would be till dinner. St. Dominic's was just such a church as old City magnates should have worshipped and grown rich in. The place had a look of tarnished bullion and dingy guineas; it made one think of the dark corners of old counting-rooms. On the walls and over the chancel, upward-gazing saints aspired with the faith of long-gone ages. The glad singing of the choristers and the murmurings of the people arose incessantly; from the tablets upon the walls the past gave testimony. There, with the dark wilderness of London trade without, the people knelt and worshipped in the same old place which had been a landmark to their believing fathers.

After church the curate used to guide me through all sorts of strange lanes and arcades, and openings, and narrow passages through which we could scarcely get abreast, to the vicarage, which was a third of a mile away, where half-a-dozen of the parsons of the neighbourhood gathered for supper. Incessant and indefatigable as he was, he yet seemed to have more time for his friends than many men who do not accomplish a fourth of his work. I took advantage of all the time I could get of him. He was always to be found after church on Sunday when the same group that gathered at the vicarage came to him to lunch. These meetings were marked by a friendship and abandon rare, I should have supposed, among Englishmen. This we owed to the hospitality of the curate's spirit, and his laugh, which, I think, was one of the most delightful I ever heard. He possessed a most capacious nature. His humour, of which he had a great deal, was just like his frame, large and ruddy. He was from the farmer class; and, it seemed to me, that he had in his blood the jollity of a hundred Christmas Eves, and in his voice the warmth and volume of centuries of roaring Yule-logs upon the hearth. He had perfect health; he was three-and-thirty, indeed, but he had that other youth—the youth of purity and simplicity. On Sundays he usually came back from church in great spirits. His talk with his clerical friends ran upon parish matters, the peculiarities of some familiar people, an odd answer of a charity scholar to a question in the catechism, or what had been seen and heard among the poor during the week. For instance (this was told me in a subdued voice, as if to apologise for its profanity), the curate had called upon a poor girl who had lost her baby. He tried to comfort her, and told her that it was better off where it was. She was inconsolable; but when he reminded her that it had gone to Heaven, she said "yes" (sobbing), that she believed it was a "bloody little angel." I mention this to show the strength of the soil from which these men drew their nutriment. Their conversation was full of fact and personal experience; but the wit and pleasure, the "sweet insanity" to which the company attained when their minds were the clearest and kindest, they owed to the patronage and hospitality of the host The freedom and perfect unselfishness of the parson provoked the humour of his guests to the very limit of audacity; indeed, at times, to the border of delirium.

This pale photograph is all I have with which to reproduce his modesty, his efficiency, his goodness, his friendship, his humour. Even these words—a hieroglyphical sort of suggestion of him rather than of definition—may bring him into trouble, should they find their way across the ocean. The ladies at the vicarage, where we used to sup on Sunday evenings after service, used to tease him sorely. Indeed, that was the way they took to testify the warm regard in which they held the curate. They had rather a handle against him in the great devotion of certain old ladies in the parish. These old people could not help testifying their love of him, and not very skilful in expressing themselves, would make use of epithets rather more fond than accurate. Expressions meant for parsons of the honeyed or pallid and ascetic sort sat rather absurdly upon his broad shoulders. Then there were certain good and pretty women who used to persecute this devout man and worthy servant by recalling these compliments in his presence. Thus he was never permitted to forget that he had been called "the handsomest curate in Wolverton." Perhaps they may find something in my encomiums to tease him about. I can see him after church on Sunday evenings at the vicarage, indulging deep draughts of beer, and very busy at the cold chicken, amid gusts of his own laughter and expostulation, exclaiming that a certain friend of his is a "blasted Yankee," "a heretic," &c.

People in England do not run together so much

by churches as in this country. There is the broad division between the Establishment and the Dissenters, much broader than that between any two American denominations, though the line is by no means so marked as it once was. But you find comparatively very little association by particular church societies. In the West-End there is none at all; in the less fashionable parts of London the Church is a sort of focus for the congregation, but to no such degree as in America. They have nothing like our Sunday schools, about which the young people in an American town and village get together, and which, in their own minds, they associate much more intimately with cider and hickory nuts than with the catechism. Sunday schools in England are entirely for the poor. The original object was to teach children who could not go to school during the week. Of the bright and attractive gatherings of pretty children and happy people among us they have no idea. The Sunday school here is so national and peculiar an institution, that I wonder it has not got into literature. The number of people, the country through, who have recollections of them, must be very great. In the days when school discipline was severer than at present, a boy's reason for liking them was that they did not "lick" and "keep in." But the man who looks back upon those festivals will remember some impressions more exalted and mystical than any he has known since. There was a pale little girl, with a demeanour of almost severe purity, and a face quite grave and intense, who, on Sunday mornings, was hid from him too often by intervening and constantly interrupting heads and bonnets. The breeze that swung the branches into the open windows, rattled the Bible leaves, and blew a skein of her yellow hair over her temples. Then there was a boy of fifteen, who was the secretary, and who wore coat-tails, and who was a very great personage. With book in hand and pencil behind his ear, he went among the girls and gathered pennies, and received the offering of the pale little girl, apparently unconscious that she was unlike the others. This boy was marshal, and wore a rosette on excursions, and when a missionary came to address the school, he rose and moved a vote of thanks. Wild and thrilling eminence! There was but one unpleasant thing about the Sunday school, that to-morrow was Monday, and that the sight of the pale little girl, and the pleasant hubbub about Jonah and Elijah, would be exchanged for the long, dark school-room, and the desks and the black-boards, and "What place was celebrated for its manufactures?" and "What place for the intelligence of its inhabitants?" the odious smell of slate and slate-pencil; the master's ruler over the hands and his cane over the legs.

But Sunday schools have of late years become much prettier places than they were fifteen or twenty years ago. At present they fit them up with fountains, nice furniture, and warm-coloured carpets, and the walls are decorated with mottoes and texts of Scripture in red, blue, and gilt. They sing sweetly and heartily, and the conversational hubbub of voices is bright and exhilarating. The confusion of tongues and subjects, when one sits in the midst of it, is agreeable. A little boy near you spells out, "Go to the ant, thou sluggard." In the Bible class a young collegian of an investigating and somewhat sceptical turn is confounding the wisdom of his simple-minded teacher, who is really in much awe of him, expostulates with his erudition and logical superiority, and warns him that too much learning has made him mad. Over the way the bears are devouring the boys who mocked Elisha; while a fair little group of girls to your left are taking down the priests of Baal to a destruction which they and their teacher in a rather matter-of-course and apathetic manner appear to approve. Considering that so many human beings are cut to pieces, the look of mild and tacit acquiescence in the young teacher's countenance is rather dreadful, and it is somewhat strange that the scholars should inspect each other's dresses, and exchange confidences, and that their faces should fall into absent and far-away expressions.

They have none of these pretty things in England. I once attended a sort of Sunday school in the loft of a warehouse down by the river, where some bargees were taught. The young boatmen walked in in single file with an enormous clamping of boots, which must have been wooden, and an expression upon their countenances of an intention to behave with great decorum. They knelt down much as you would suppose a row of Egyptian obelisks to do, and when down you wished that they would never attempt to get up again. One young man did continue kneeling some moments longer than was necessary. He arose with as much haste as possible, and the whole of them, as a matter of course, immediately crammed their handkerchiefs down their throats (or whatever in a bargee's wardrobe corresponds to a handkerchief), and by this pantomime expressed their readiness to choke rather than violate propriety. I suppose that all British Sunday schools are modifications of this one. As the children who compose them are taken altogether from the very poorest, a look of squalor and dirt must be, I imagine, inseparable from them.

St. Dominic's had no Sunday schools like ours, yet the young people of the church had some exceedingly pleasant ways of spending time. For instance, they had dances during the Christmas holidays in the school-room of the church, to the great scandal of some of the neighbouring parishes. A small sum was charged for admission. The room was prettily decorated with holly, evergreen, and ivy; and all the young people of the church came and danced. Over this little realm, hid in the heart of London trade, the vicar's wife, a person of much sense and beauty, exercised a pleasant rule. Most of the young men had rather a half-baked look; the best of them, it was easy to see, were not quite done. But my experience is that gentle and refined and lady-like women are of no class at all; you find them everywhere. For centuries the beauty of London women has been famous. These young ladies, indeed, were not quite like the slight, pale slips, and faintly tinted blue-bells of the West-End. Bloom and zone they possessed in abundance. The faces of many of them were exceedingly comely. They had health, spirits, good-nature, and much freedom and humour. St. Dominic's was very high, or very broad, or both, or neither, I forget which; but, at any rate, it occupied just that theological attitude which a church may hold and give charity balls to the young people. At such times the school-room was too small, and they secured a hall in the neighbourhood. These assemblages, I think, attracted rather a higher class of people than the dances in the school-room. Thither came the most devout and charitable ladies of the parish. You may fancy how pleasant it was; the church at Philippi gave me the right hand of fellowship. I was permitted to waltz with Priscilla, to gallop with Lydia, and to *balancez* and turn not a few of the chief women in the lancers.

St. Dominic's, it will be seen, practised a very agreeable type of Christianity. It must not be imagined, however, that this religion was in very general vogue. I heard a number of elderly people say that they never heard of such things in their lives as a dance in a church school-room. But a great many strange things have come to pass which elderly people never heard of. It really seems at present that everybody is tolerated except the Evangelicals. There are in England at present a great many kinds of people, and a great many kinds of belief. They have a strong, ably expressed, and respectable unbelief, like which we have nothing in America; and lying oddly by the side of it is a good deal of what might be termed "religion as a matter of course." Thus, it is mentioned in the Blue Books that certain children in the agricultural regions cannot tell who made them ; yet this is not to be wondered at, when so many of the learned professors in the universities say they don't know. As a specimen of the diversity of opinion one meets with, a young lady once told me that she saw no reason to believe in the immortality of the soul ; and that women, she thought, were religious because they had nothing else to do. The next day a young curate assured me that on no account could he marry an Evangelical girl; though this austerity, I fancy, was a reminiscence of a severe youth which time and nature had mollified. (He promised, by-the-way, that he would take me to call upon an "Evangelical girl," which he never did.) Between these extremes there is obviously room for some shades of opinion. Yet widely diverse as are the notions of men, all alike receive the heritage which the strong religious moods of early England have bequeathed them. They yet have the churches and the universities, St. Paul's, the Abbey, and Magdalen cloisters. There yet remain abodes of solitude and emotion which no modern hands can imitate, where men in mighty cities can retire apart for an hour from the crowd, and dust, and turmoil.

The night of my arrival in London I stopped at a hotel not far from Westminster. It was raining during the evening, and I did not go out, but sat before the grate in the smoking-room, strangely reflecting upon the strange, dark, new, old world about me. It was one of those large hotels to which people go who know nothing about London, and I had dined in a hushed and stately dining-hall instead of the dingy little coffee-room one should always seek. I was disappointed with the arid elegance of my surroundings, and began to fear that the world I was to enter upon the morrow might be as vain and modern. There was a young clergyman sitting near me, with whom I entered into talk. He was the rector of a parish somewhere in Shropshire, of which he told me the name, and it had an extremely pleasant country sound. (The reader will perhaps think me impressible, but why should I tell him of the stupid people I met?) I had never met a man, it seemed to me, with a manner and spirit more refined, and when afterwards I had an opportunity to know him better, that impression was fixed and strengthened. His countenance and behaviour united gentleness and purity, softness and dignity. In the course of the conversation he spoke of the Abbey, and as he was modestly and kindly communicative, I got from him a good deal about it. He took a pencil and sketched me some hints of its architectural history; and he told me this story, which is perhaps familiar to many of my readers, but was new to me. Ages ago a clear stream watered the grassy margin of the river, where now the brown, viscid wave of the Thames laves its stone walls and embankments. Once at night a boatman saw upon the bank a man who beckoned him to come nearer. He rowed him across the stream to where the Abbey stood. The figure entered, and immediately the church was filled with light and music, and singing angels. It was St. Peter who came to possess and consecrate his Cathedral. When my acquaintance retired he proposed that we should attend the ten o'clock services at the Abbey the next morning. "They have every day," he said, "a morning and afternoon service. It is well to have some place in the heart of the city where one can be apart with one's God." The manner of the young clergyman was constrained and diffident; I can convey no impression of the gentleness and purity with which these words were uttered.

The next morning we went to the Abbey. I have never been since so distinctly conscious of the mood of which it was the expression—if it be not presumption to talk of distinctness upon such a subject. I felt in the authors of that work a sense of that strong exclusion which possesses all artists in their clearest moments. Had the builders not had the sympathy of the multitude, these were emotions which, when brought in contact with an alien and astonished atmosphere, would have appeared how wild, how strange! They could not have survived a day which did not comprehend them. But the aspiration and exultation had been changed to the stone of the solid globe. The thoughts of the builders may now fly hither and thither, the builders die and their visions with them, but still that dream entranced remains ; the towers yet linger, the arches exult, the saints aspire; so I thought when first those aisles and ascending vaults were revealed to me, and when, with the pious few gathered under its canopy, I first heard the rejoicing of the choristers.

Two Visits to Oxford.

A NOTION, I believe, still prevails very generally that Oxford and Cambridge are the universities of the English aristocracy. It is to the novelists that we owe this impression. Years ago, these universities were very much such places as Bulwer and Thackeray have painted them. But they have altered, and there has been nothing in their recent literature to mark the change. They still exist to a large portion of the public as elegant and aristocratic as ever. To the imagination of the English shop-girl, Oxford and Cambridge are yet peopled by a race of the most delightful heroes, who breakfast in velvet, who have valets and tigers and tandems, who ride and shoot and borrow each other's money, who are aristocratically lavish and aristocratically hard up.

Now, on the contrary, the real Oxford does not resemble this conception in the least, and at first sight, perhaps, the social life of the place is even plainer and more commonplace than we should observe it to be on closer acquaintance. One has scarcely stepped into the streets before he meets numbers of well-behaved, modest youth, walking by twos and threes, not in droves, as students patrol the streets of an American university town. There cannot be found in Europe, I imagine, a more well-conducted, orderly generation of young men. The most of them are from the middle classes and are upon limited incomes. The average allowance of an Oxford undergraduate is not more than 1,200 dollars, upon which, of course, magnificence is out of the question. The number of clergymen's sons is very great, and these, as a rule, are poor.

It is thought that a man can live nicely and entertain moderately on 1,500 dollars. The undergraduates have a dinner "in Hall" of fish, roast, and sweet, and at dinner they usually drink beer instead of wine. They have opportunities for luxury and elegance in their breakfasts, which they make very inviting. They brew at Oxford a claret cup with which nothing of the same kind one tastes anywhere else can be compared. The young men are exceedingly kind and hospitable, and they possess a modesty which absolutely humiliates one.

An English youth, as I saw him in the army or at the universities, who is sufficiently well born to have all the advantages of breeding, and sufficiently removed from exceptional fortune not to be tempted to folly and nonsense, has the very perfection of behaviour. He has, besides, very nearly the perfection of right feeling towards his associates, which cannot be said of him a few years later. I knew some of the undergraduates of Christ Church and Baliol. Under their guidance I went the walks of the universities, and especially remember a bath in the river, to which I consented under the impression that it would be rather an interesting and romantic action, and would furnish a pretty souvenir, but I found the wave of the Isis much too cold for comfort. Christ Church is rather a college for the sons of rich men; it is not considered, I believe, that they do much work there. Baliol is one of the working colleges—those which take the honours. The talk of the Baliol men, I thought, ran rather more to books and literature than the conversation at Christ Church. This was possibly due to the fact that a Christ Church man was to give a ball that week, which was naturally the topmost matter of interest among the men of his college. At Baliol, when the pewter cup of beer went round, of which each took a cool swig in succession, we spoke of matters which are rarely discussed with interest except at universities and by very young men. We talked of the poets, and I remember one young gentleman's enthusiasm swept him into reciting a half dozen lines of Greek.

The pride in scholarship, and the respect for it, I am told, are very much on the decline. Firsts and double-firsts are not held in such esteem as formerly. One hears it said that the boating and cricket men have thrown the reading men into the shade. A good cricketer is asked everywhere, and talked and written about, and pushed in society. Years ago many good stories were told of the extravagant regard which successful prize-men received from the universities. It was said that a senior wrangler from Cambridge happened to enter a theatre in London at the same time with the Queen, and, hearing the plaudits, placed his hand gracefully over his heart, and bowed his acknowledgments to the audience. The old fashion, no doubt, had its absurdities, as all fashions have; but, upon the whole, it was more reasonable than the present one. We are mistaken if we fancy that it is mere "dig" and memory which makes the successful man in a university examination. It requires not only persistence, but ability, intelligence, and self-possession. Of course where many work, the victory must be to him who works most intelligently. The scholar and the boating man must equally guard against over-training; and at the hour of examination the danger of losing one's head is very much greater than in a boat-race. The stake is so great that the strain of the contest seems a cruel one for very young men to undergo. If they win, they have a competency for the rest of their days—a thing to be appreciated in England, where a living is so very hard to make. All the mothers and cousins are waiting breathlessly for the issue. Such competition must, I fancy, impart an almost abnormal stimulus to the moral qualities. In the faces of the stronger men one observes some "silent rages," which the intensity of the struggle has nursed. Why such men should have less consideration than a cricketer or a stroke-oar one can hardly see. A strong back and good legs are fine gifts, no doubt; but it is hard to understand why their possessor should be so petted and fêted, should have his picture in the illustrated papers, and have his disorders telegraphed over two continents. The vignettes in the papers appear especially absurd. Why should boating men have pictures made of their faces? They should, it would seem, stand on their heads and have their legs taken.

It was during Commemoration week that I first visited Oxford. The exercises consist of the conferring of degrees upon distinguished persons, and the recital of prize poems in Greek, Latin, and English; and I may incidentally remark, that at no ball or party in England do you ever see so many pretty girls as at a university commemoration. The same is true, however, of college celebrations everywhere; girls have a way of looking their prettiest at them. The degree conferred upon strangers at Oxford is that of Doctor of Civil Law. It is not supposed that a man should know anything of law to be a D.C.L. Critics, poets, politicians, inventors, noblemen, for being noblemen, are doctored. The first commemoration I saw was at the installation of Lord Salisbury. The candidates were marshalled up the hall from the door in single file, all dressed in red gowns. The Professor of Civil Law, Mr. Bryce, introduced each in a Latin speech, which contained some happy characterisation. The Chancellor then addressed the candidate in another Latin speech, applying to him some complimentary expressions; the bar was raised, and he shook the candidate by the hand, who sat down a D.C.L. Of course, as always happens in England, there was a throng of people of rank who went ahead of abler men. The cheering of the undergraduates, however, went some distance towards equalising things. The men who received the warmest applause were Liddon, the famous preacher, and Arnold, the poet. When it came to the latter gentleman's turn, all young Oxford in the galleries went wild. They made a prodigious cheering; the young men's enthusiasm was enough to stir some generous blood in the most sluggish veins. Of course, Mr. Arnold's comparative youthfulness had much to do with it, and his recent attacks upon the Dissenters had endeared him to the clergymen's sons in the galleries. The Chancellor, who had been throwing about his *issimes* profusely among people of whom I at least had never heard, contented himself with calling Mr. Arnold, *vir ornatissime*, or some other opprobrious epithet—which, as one of Mr. Arnold's many admirers, I felt called upon to resent. I understood afterwards, however, that Lord Salisbury had considered the propriety of addressing him as *O lucidissime et dulcissime* (most light and most sweet), which, I suppose, would scarcely have done. He did joke, though, in one case; he addressed the editor of the "Edinburgh Review" as *vir doctissime, in republica litterarum potentissime,* and at that everybody was amused. The incident gives one a high idea of the power which inheres in reserve, dignity, and position. A cabinet minister, by congratulating an editor upon his formidableness in the republic of letters, creates more merriment than could a harlequin by throwing his body into twenty contortions.

The bad behaviour of the undergraduates in the gallery on these occasions is famous. I was present at two commemorations, and can testify to the power of lung and the great good humour and animal spirits of the British youth. At the last commemoration they kept up an incessant howl from the beginning to the end. I cannot say much for the wit, though, I believe, they do sometimes hit upon something worth recording. When Longfellow was made D.C.L. an undergraduate proposed, "Three cheers for the red man of the West," which, I am told, Mr. Longfellow thought very good. But, of course, wit and originality are just as rare among yelling boys as in synods and parliaments. The scant wit is supplemented by the more widely diffused qualities of impudence and vocal volume. When the Vice-Chancellor, Dr. Liddell, of Liddell and Scott's Dictionary (the accent of his name, by-the-way, is not upon the last syllable), was reading a Latin address, some one would call out, "Now construe." A man who violated the canons of dress by appearing in a white coat was fairly stormed out of the place. He stood it for an hour or so, during which he was addressed: "Take off that coat, sir." "Go out, sir." "*Won't* you go at once?" "Ladies, request him to leave." "Doctor Brown, won't *you* put that man out?" (Then, in a conversational and moderate tone), "Just put your hand upon his shoulder and lead him out." After an hour of it, the man withdrew. Each successive group of ladies was cheered as it came in. The young men would exclaim: "Three cheers for the ladies in blue." "Three cheers for the ladies in white, brown, red, grey," &c. The poor fellows who read the prize odes and essays were dreadfully bullied. One young man recited an English poem, of which I could not catch the burden, but from the manner of its delivery I should say that it must have been upon the saddest subject that ever engaged the muse of mortal. His physiognomy and his tone of voice alike expressed the dismal and the disconsolate. I think that possibly the extreme sadness of his manner may have been induced by the reception rather than the matter of his poem. They cat-called, hooted him, and laughed immeasurably at him. One young gentleman with an eye-glass leaned over the gallery, and in a colloquial tone inquired, "My friend, is that the refrain that hastened the decease of the old cow?" In the intervals of the horrible hootings, I-could only now and then catch a word like "breeze" or "trees." By-and-by the galleries caught the swing of the poet's measure, and kept time to his cadences with their feet, and with a rhythmical roar of their voices. It was too painful to laugh at. One felt so for the poor fellow, and more still for his mother and sisters, who, I am sure, were there. I was particularly glad to notice among the men who last year were compelled to face the music, a man who the year before had been especially energetic in the galleries.

To see an English university, one should look at it from the don's side rather than the undergraduates'. Undergraduates are of exceedingly little importance. The dons are the essentials of university life; the students are its transient and unimportant incidents. At Yale, when we were juniors, we thought ourselves of consequence. We considered a senior greater than a professor, and the tutors we pretended to hold in no esteem at all. The purpose of the founders of the University of Oxford, as one dispirited and conservative old gentleman told me, was originally not study alone, but study and devotion. The colleges were associations of men who gave their lives to learning and religion. The education of youth was rather an afterthought and an incident. Whether or not the present state of things at Oxford and Cambridge is the result of tradition, it is certainly true that the fellows and masters of the colleges constitute the universities. At Cambridge I had letters to two of the Fellows of Trinity; and at Oxford I was the guest for a week of a friend who was a fellow of Oriel. The spirit and social atmosphere of the two universities seemed to me very much the same; almost any statement which might be true of the society of either would be true of the other.

A Fellow, as everybody knows, passes a good examination, and for the rest of his life, or until marriage, draws from the university an income of from 1,000 to 1,500 dollars. For this he is under no obligation to return any labour. Those who reside at the universities are usually tutors or lecturers, and for these services of course receive extra pay. On marriage they are compelled to resign their fellowships. The men who wish to marry, obtain, if they can, livings in the Church, school-inspectorships, or appointments under government. Recently the universities have been pressing the abolition of the restriction upon marriage, and expecting it from every successive parliament. It is both pleasant and painful to think of the number of interesting young couples who at this moment are waiting for a word from the British Government. A very pretty tale one might make of it. The story of another Evangeline, waiting through long years upon the slow steps of legislation, and rising each morning to scan with eager eyes the parliamentary proceedings, might form a good subject for a play or a poem. I examined very few of the considerations in favour of the reform. This one presents itself, however—men are always strangely tempted to what is forbidden them ; celibacy may not be so irksome, if they know they may marry when they choose. Upon the other side I heard a bachelor urge that the university would cease to be such an equal, reasonable, sensible place as it has been heretofore. The women would introduce discord. The wife of a Head would no doubt think herself above a poor tutor's, and would give herself airs.

Were it not for the peculiar and easily explained susceptibility of college tutors, the circumstances of their bachelor life are so delightful that one might wonder that even matrimony can tempt them away from it. The physical life is looked after very well. The dinners are fair and the lodgings comfortable. The bachelor can do there what is difficult to do elsewhere : he can live well and dine in pleasant company. He is not solitary as at a club, and the company of congenial men who have the same interests with himself makes the commons' dinner infinitely better than any *table d'hôte.* The dons' rooms are of all degrees of comfort and elegance. Some of them are very bare ; others are pretty and well furnished. The rooms of men who have been some time at the university, and who have a taste for elegance, grow to be pretty; and a pleasantly-arranged room, I believe, must always be the result of time. At Merton College, Oxford, I saw an apartment of which the whole front had been made into a bow-window, facing upon a green and humid quadrangle. Its occupant, I remember, showed me, among his curiosities, a side-board of the 17th century, on which was carved in very bold relief a good part of the events of Genesis. There was a figure of the Lord, about as long as your finger, walking in the garden; and Adam and Eve and the Serpent were engaged in conversation about the Tree of the Knowledge of Good and Evil. Adam, strange to say, was accompanied by a dog of some choice breed, which smelt about his heels in a rather clumsy wooden manner, but very much as fallen canine nature is yet in the habit of doing. Such elegance and curiousness are unusual, I suppose, though many of the rooms are cozy and inviting. The ceilings are low, and low ceilings are warm and pleasant. One is delighted with the sense of the ancient atmosphere, the ample grate, the books upon the shelves and strewn about the tables.

At Cambridge I left my cards and letters, and in walking about the town missed seeing J——, of Trinity, who had called in my absence, but I chanced to meet the dean of one of the smaller colleges, whom I had known in London, and I accepted his invitation to his college. I went with him the pretty walk behind the colleges, and, reaching his room, found there several of the tutors who had strolled in, and were sitting in the dusk before the grate, waiting for dinner. The dining-hall of the college was small and dimly lighted. There were but three or four of the Fellows present, and we sat together upon a raised platform. An undergraduate read a long grace in Latin. I sat with my back to the wall, so that I could look over the Fellows down upon the tables, dim and candle-lit, where the young men dined. The fewness of the undergraduates, and the quiet and dark of the hall gave one a feeling something like that which children have when huddled under a big umbrella. Sitting in talk with these intelligent, unaffected scholars, and having one's heart warmed by their genial converse and kind attention, and with one's only distraction to peep into the dim and quiet ends of the room, how blessed seemed these men's occupations, how pleasant the tenor of their lives; how attractive appeared the comfort, the poetry, and solid happiness there is in learning! The hall at Trinity is, I believe, the great place to see. "If they ask you to dine there, mind you go," I was told. But who does not know the pleasure of finding beauties and curiosities of which the almanacs say nothing! I liked to think that the earth contained so happy a spot as this dim hall of ——— College, unpraised of men and unheralded by the guide-books. I was more diverted with the old side-board at Merton than with the Tower of London.

The next morning the Dean and myself accepted an invitation to breakfast from J——, of Trinity. We climbed up one of those dark, narrow, perpendicular winding staircases, and knocked upon his door, and our host came out to meet us. He introduced me to two or three others whom he had invited. It was raining, I remember, and the windows of his room looked down upon a dripping garden (garden is the name given to a lawn planted with trees), and a little arched bridge which crossed a stream like a mill-race. The drops fell rapidly against the window-panes, and it was dark and warm in the large, low, old room where we breakfasted. My host's conversation was light and witty, and the talk of the table ran much to politics, and that pleasantest and most instructive kind of discourse, gossip. A good deal was said of education, which is one of the most pressing political questions for Great Britain. One gentleman, who was a school-inspector, had been driving about England, looking at the private schools everywhere along his route, and examining the teachers and scholars. With the exception of the examination, it struck me that this must be a very pleasant occupation.

There were present at this breakfast several men who, I was told, were very clever; and again, as elsewhere in Cambridge and Oxford, was I struck with a quality of theirs, which if I praise they may laugh at me—I mean their modesty. Some of them were even diffident. It was a pleasure to look at these men, and think, "You know ever so much about international law, and *you* about the Greek philosophy, and nobody knows what *you* can tell us about the particles." My host was a lecturer upon Plato, I believe. We sat together for an hour after breakfast, and I fell to admiring audibly his circumstances and employments. Our conversation was upon topics not usually touched upon by men on the first day of an acquaintance. One of the drawbacks of travel is that natural delicacy which forbids men who are strangers from speaking upon any but trivial subjects. The necessity is sometimes rather hard upon travellers, who are always strangers. But I remember the Trinity lecturer making such a remark as this—that no course of philosophical reading ever gave satisfactory opinions to anybody. Still, it is very well to have tested for oneself the vanity of such a way of getting at the truth. But it is not to be expected that they would appreciate their advantages; scarcely anybody does. My host walked with me about the colleges, and promised, if I stayed, that I should see an old gentleman who had been Lord Byron's tutor when that young nobleman was an undergraduate at Trinity.

At Oxford I was for a week the guest of a friend who was a Fellow of Oriel. An Oriel Fellowship has always been, I am told, the undergraduate's blue-ribbon; and I presume that the men I met there were very excellent specimens of Oxford. The undergraduates had left the university, and the Fellows of Oriel dined, not in hall, but in the wine-room. A curious feature of the meal, the grace, has been, I believe, incorrectly given by visitors. Before dinner they say "*Benedictus benedicat*," and after dinner—*i.e.*, just before dessert—somebody drops his head in the middle of the talk and says, "*Benedicto benedicatur.*" The room is hung round with pictures of the ancient and recent worthies of the college. A fine and large likeness of Clough looked down upon the warm and pleasant scene. This sort of living, compared with the only bachelor modes of existence I had ever known—a club, a boarding-house, or a hotel—seemed perfection. And if the old wainscoted room and the company of the genial scholars was so pleasing, what did I think one evening when, dining at Merton College, famed for the beauty of its gardens, coffee was served in a rustic seat on the lawn, and, as the summer evening came down upon the grass and the still trees, and a star or two came out and brightened, and the towers over us and about us grew grayer and darker, we sat and talked, and listened far into the twilight?

In a week's stay about Oxford I saw it in many forms and moods. An Oxford quadrangle is the hoariest and most ancient spectacle in my experience. Shut up in one of them at the time of sun-down the impression is particularly strong. One feels the planet to have aged. I found it difficult to conceive that a scene yet strong with the strength of Nature remained anywhere in the world. It was hard to think that beyond the swelling and sinking Atlantic the blue line of the Alleghany trembled over the quiet harvests of a familiar valley, or that the stream of the yellow Missouri drowned with disconsolate floods his black slimy islands of sand.

Some of the quadrangles were very gray and

sombre; others were warm and happy. In the cloisters of Magdalen they have found the flower which best harmonises with the associations of the place. It is the wild rose. Upon a mid-summer afternoon, when Oxford is deserted—when no feet but your own are heard in the cloisters—when the blue air of the quadrangle is warmed to the fill by the sun—there is that in the odour of the flower of wild, yet sweet, of gay, yet yearning, which harmonises well with the spongy turf, with the moist air thrilled by the sunshine, with the cold recesses of the cloister and the benign silence with which the scene regards your footfall.

The character for learning of the men I met at the universities stands, I suppose, as high as that of the same class of men anywhere in the world. It is a pleasure to me to dwell upon their candour and kindness. I discovered scarcely anything to find fault with. "We grow a very disagreeable specimen of prig here," said one. I did not see him. Here and there I met a man whose playfulness had a somewhat learned flavour and whose speeches might, when repeated, have had a sound of pedantry, but the awkwardness was accompanied by a simplicity which made it rather attractive. I must say, though, that the wit was a little wordy—but that is true of the wit of young college tutors everywhere; their jokes may be said to have extension, their jests and quips remind one of the gambols of a Newfoundland pup. The older men, where they were not more solemn, had rather more pith and point. But the wit of scholars is apt to be diluted, just as is that of the man of fashion, though from a different cause. The wit of the man of fashion shares the general feebleness of his nature; that of the scholar is poor because he does not see enough of life; because the situations in which he is an actor or a looker-on are not sufficiently numerous, various, and rapidly successive.

What especially strikes the visitor at the universities is their way of speaking the unadulterated truth; it does not occur to them that anything else should be spoken. They have their pretenders and humbugs in England just as here—men who live and thrive by the inevitable folly and inattention of the mass of the community. Some poor offspring of a lucky talent and a lucky opportunity wins applause and place and profit with scarcely a struggle. Some light creature gets the start of this tremendous world, and is swept onward like a leaf. Oxford and Cambridge are the places to hear these men called by their right names. It is just as well that most people do not indulge in such plain speaking, for most people would be apt to be mistaken. But at the universities there are many thinking, educated men, whose opinions are tolerably apt to be correct. They are very little troubled with that charity which will say no ill of your neighbour because the report of it may come to your neighbour's ear. They have no axes to grind, no ulterior aims, no policies. One evening at Oxford a well-known name was mentioned, and the whole company at once agreed that he was an ass. That was my own opinion; but had I mentioned it among people more polite and circumspect, I should have been thought, if not a jealous and deprecatory person, at least a very rash one—perhaps one of those envious detractors who go about tearing the reputations of the great and good. The man was certainly dull and talkative, yet he deserved respect of a kind. There was an acerbity, however, in the comment which his folly did not quite explain. Why should they so go out of the way to abuse a comparatively unimportant man for merely being an ass? This point was naïvely met by one ingenuous young accuser, who said, "After all, the only thing I have against him is that he's a successful man."

English writers upon this country have given us the impression that their scholars are less men of the world than our own. I found the young men at Oxford and Cambridge very greatly interested in matters outside their universities. Many of them, I thought, were piqued by the social power which the aristocracy still retains in England, for no men are better placed than themselves to see how belated is the entire face of their society. Not a few of them have aspirations for political careers. Many are barristers and have chambers in London, some few conducting cases, but many more waiting for them. For those who are only students and citizens of the world, the greatest city in Europe is but two hours away. It is they who get most out of university life. They may infest, if they choose, those old quadrangles of Oxford for a lifetime; the ends of Europe are within two days of them. The physical man and the eating, drinking, and sleeping man are well enough cared for. They have the great libraries, and the constant society of cultivated men in such numbers that they may look about among themselves for suitable acquaintance. They have for a home one of the most beautiful places in the world. There is scarcely a happy circumstance of a scholar's life which fortune and the generous wisdom of the men who have been through centuries the custodians of their university have denied them.

The British Upper Class in Fiction.

"NOT you, but the house derides me," said the wolf to the kid in the fable. This is the answer which society makes to any insolent or arrogant individual who happens to be out of its reach. Fortunate men everywhere are apt to fall into the kid's mistake; and of all swells, none cherishes the delusion so honestly as an Englishman. He stands there protected in that *insouciance* which the novelists admire, and which he himself deems the consummate result of history and human progress, by defences which are none of his making. The radical claim, the fundamental distinction of an Englishman of the upper class is, that no man can get the better of him in *hauteur*. The neighbourhood of the most oppressive or confusing personality will run off him like water. He will flush as he passes no man; no man can give him two fingers. Should by any chance his bosom acknowledge impression or trepidation, his exterior shall be calm as stone. And he is proud to think that this gift of his is not the accident of his station or his circumstances, but is an inherent virtue of his own, of which adverse fortune cannot rob him. He may be deprived of health, money, and friends; he may be baffled and beaten here, and lost hereafter; but it is his belief and consolation that the time can never come when he may be snubbed.

To this it may be said, that the courage which confronts a future or a possible evil is a very easy one. Difficulty, until we meet it face to face, is an unknown quantity. It is x; when really upon us, it becomes $a + b$. He who is in the midst of the difficulty he challenged from a distance, may with perfect consistency retire, claiming that when he made the engagement, he had not sufficient data to go upon. He agreed to encounter x, not $a + b$.

Undoubtedly the qualities which constitute the

distinction in the swell are precisely *not* the qualities which constitute success in the great struggle of man for subsistence. The "survivors" of Mr. Herbert Spencer have succeeded by alert attention, rather than by an elegant inattention. The monkey that saw the apple first got it; the chimpanzee that first saw the wild cat was the first to get away from him. In the "incoherent" ages, when one man met in the forest another who was carrying a sword or a spear, he did not saunter by, relying upon his own unconscious majesty, and the impressibility of his adversary, as a protection against a blow in the back of the head. He was the best man who had the most and the quickest perceptions, rather than he who had the fewest and the slowest.

But whatever may have been true of those remote and uncertain ages, in society, as we know it, the alert, attentive man plainly gets ahead of the inattentive one. A certain suavity and deference in his dealings with others will not hurt him. He cannot ignore the man out of whom he makes money. He cannot snub a client, a customer, or a patient with impunity.

The swell, therefore, whom adverse fortune compels to take his chances with other men, has either to fail, or to relinquish his superb behaviour, and to change his principle of elegant unconsciousness into one of alert attention. He may say that he will die first, which would perhaps be the more heroic and graceful exit from the difficulty, providing he died at once. But he thus registers himself among the defeated and fails—the very thing it was the boast of his ancestors that they did not do. Should he happen to have hostages to fortune, in the shape of wife and children, the complexion of his case would be entirely altered. To take defeat for himself would be his right; to accept it for those dependent upon him would be quite another thing. It is pretty plain, then, that the swell is very much in the position of the kid upon the house-top. If he were a lawyer's clerk, of course these fine ways would have to cease. If he were on the staff of a popular weekly, and had to dance in the liveliest paragraphs under the whip of the managing editor, or the proprietors, or the public, he would find his unconsciousness and *hauteur* very inconvenient. He would, no doubt, consider the editor a demagogue, an inaccurate, semi-honest, and wholly uneducated person; would gnash his teeth in secret over the failure of the proprietors duly to appreciate their own vulgarity, and would heartily despise the silly public; but when this inadequate revenge had been taken, there would be nothing left for him to do.

It was very easy to see that, as a matter of fact, the young Englishman of the class of which I am speaking did change his manners as soon as his circumstances changed. Men of precisely the same claims of birth had a very different behaviour. Those who had to make their way acquired a more eager, and, as a rule, a more complaisant manner than their luckier cousins. Even diplomatists and private secretaries to heads of departments were evidently alive to, and anxious to conciliate the good opinions of others. At the clubs it was not difficult to pick out, from their more alert behaviour, the men whose fortunes were capable of improvement, and who were on the look-out to better them. In a word, when in England, I saw that a swell, so soon as he perceives that his distinctions do not pay, relinquishes them.

It will be seen that these distinctions appeal for admiration to persons in a certain middle condition of education. Those who appreciate such graces to the full must be somewhat civilised and yet somewhat immature. A degree of impressibility in the men who look on is the condition of the exercise of the swell's talent. What sort of impression would *insouciance* make upon a hungry tiger? Nor would it impress an educated and acute man who insists upon submitting reverie to the test of definition and criticism. It is to the shop-boy, and the writer for the spring annual, that such graces appeal.

The aristocracy has received, from time to time, very various treatment at the hands of literature. The writers of the age of Queen Anne—a keen and critical race—never gave them any very respectful consideration. Later in the century the novelists dealt with them in a very truthful and sensible fashion. Fielding, I remember, somewhere takes occasion to explain in a foot-note that by the "mob" he does not mean the common people, but the coarse and the ignoble in every rank. In those days the aristocracy possessed real power. When their power had come to an end, and they retained only their social precedence, the admiration of their class superiorities seems to have begun. It is a somewhat curious fact that Bulwer, Disraeli, the Kingsleys, and other writers of the last quarter of a century, have expressed an admiration for the upper classes which is new in English literature. Nothing of the kind is to be found in their great predecessors, Scott, Miss Austen, and Miss Edgeworth. The reason is, I suppose, that blessings brighten as they take their flight. The strong, whether they be good or bad, need no apology. Praise of them is rather a superfluity and an impertinence. But when power had slipped out of the hands of the upper classes, to justify the social precedence that remained, people began to look about for something of an inherent and permanent nature to admire. The gradual contraction of their privileges removed, too, the "wicked lord" from romance. His opportunities of wickedness were gone. Earls could no longer kidnap pretty women. Moreover, the rise of a powerful class of merchants, into a social prominence scarcely less than that enjoyed by them in Cromwell's time, fixed the attention of society upon the graces of the older aristocracy. The poor clergyman was glad to feel that the people who snubbed his wife were nobodies by the side of his patron. It was perhaps rather pleasant to a banker's clerk to know that there were persons before whom his own despot would have to take off his hat.

But the novel has been the peculiar literary staple of the last thirty years. The upper classes have been of great use to the playwrights and the story-tellers. The throng of tutors, governesses, and young professional men who write for the London magazines, have relied much upon the dramatic capabilities of their unequal society. The fortunate classes anywhere will always be excellent material for art, providing those classes are known to the entire society. The people like to look at them. They take the sort of pleasure in them which they experience at a *fête* or a pantomime. They wish them well, as they like the novels and the plays to end happily. The converse is also evident. So soon as these classes cease to appear fortunate they cease to be attractive. The cause of the Queen's recent unpopularity is to be found, not in her seclusion, nor in the discontent of the tradesmen who live upon Court patronage, but in the natural aversion of men to the lachrymose and the melancholy. The elegant classes here cannot be used to very great advantage, because a farmer in Illinois has a most indistinct and hazy notion of the habits of a person of fashion in New York or Boston. Moreover, here nobody knows exactly who these classes are. Abroad, this "fine" society is the most distinguished and conspicuous. Here it is the little set whose particular boast is that "nobody knows anything about it."

The reaction which followed the French Revolution; the glory to which England attained during the first third of the present century, to which she was certainly led by the upper classes, and upon which she lived until very lately; the gradual diminution of the privileges of the upper class and the sense of security from their encroachments—all these things disposed the English people to think very favourably of their aristocracy. Their impressibility and credulity and their curiosity about the aristocracy have been fed by the novelists. Many popular mistakes concerning the manners of the "great" have thus been encouraged. Thackeray even has lent countenance to the superstition that the young men are marked by a certain graceful and reckless generosity. It would seem natural that men who have assured wealth, and a station at the top of society, should exhibit towards each other a simple friendliness and an unthinking generosity, not to be found among people who are compelled to jostle and elbow each other in the struggle for subsistence. But I did not find it to be so. Lord Kew gives Jack Belsize ever so many thousand pounds. But the Lord Kews are scarce in real life. Not only is it hard to find men who give each other fortunes, but Lord Kew's spirit is not at all the spirit of the men I saw. The money they won from each other in the card-rooms and at the races, they were very anxious to get and very willing to keep. Indeed, men who are on stated allowances, as many of them were, are compelled to exercise a systematic forecast in the matter of expenses, which a man who can stretch his income by a little extra labour will scarcely take. As to the gracefully reckless kindness, the shop-boy is quite wrong in his notions upon this point. So far as I could see, they did not feel more kindly to one another than the brokers who scream each other hoarse in the New York Stock Exchange. Indeed, I believe that, as a rule, they are the most ready to help others who have most ably helped themselves.

Another of the misconceptions of the middle classes which the novelists have flattered is that their superiors are so accustomed to superiority that they have forgotten all about it. They think nothing of their distinction, it is said. On the contrary, they are always thinking about it and always talking about it. They roll it under their tongues like a sweet morsel. A friend of mine wrote to a certain very great and exalted person, asking whether we should or should not dress for a political dinner at Richmond. He answered pithily: "The snobs dress; the gentlemen don't."

I may here say that the most elegant men in dress and behaviour are not those in whom pride of lineage is strongest. Your man of stern family pride rather despises any such distinction as fine clothes and fine manners can give him. When you see an individual with his hat knocked over his eyes or his collar awry, you may know that he secretly hugs an escutcheon to his bosom with a fervour and energy of which no dandy is capable.

Thackeray's charge against the English, that they are virtue-proud, is certainly true. They think themselves the best people in the world, and after one notable exception has been made, I am inclined to agree with them. Of unkindness to foreigners upon their own shores they are unjustly accused. They are, however, defiant in their behaviour to strangers, and at this point they have been educated in another misconception. They cherish the impression that their reserve is in some way a scrutiny of the character of the individual who is a candidate for the honour of their acquaintance. But this is a mistake. They hold back till they are sure, not that he is virtuous, but that it will help them to know him. The young Englishman chooses his friends just as the young American or the young Frenchman does.

It is the way of the world to regard success and fortune as another sort of character, and here again the English are no exception to the rule. Gentle manners to the poor and dependent, and a conciliatory bearing towards acquaintance, are praised, if the man who possesses them is a person of consequence. The English say, "He knows who he is;" "Nothing can be better than he." In such a man rank seems to pass for a kind of virtue. But a seemly behaviour is not difficult to people who have no opposition. You do see men, however, in England, in whom good manners are only another sort of heroism. Life is not to them a pleasant saunter among tolerant equals and obsequious inferiors. I have known men with strong, fierce hearts and the consciousness of power and ability, who, unrecognised and in irksome and difficult positions, are yet able to conduct themselves with propriety and dignity. There are rages which come, we know not whence, and moods in which it is difficult to remember principles, yet these men learn to control them. They behave with a self-respect which does not verge upon truculence, and with a complaisance which does not approach servility.

The present tone of the fashionable novel is not that of the aristocratic romance of the early part of the century. It is not even the tone of Coningsby or Maltravers. To the story-writers of "Cornhill" and "Fraser" the nobleman is no longer picturesque, or superior, or haughty, or aquiline. The purpose of these later writers is to present him as a good deal more like most people than anybody else. The young Bohemians laugh flippantly at the "fat old duchess;" the glib governesses pour much scorn and contempt on "Lady Booby's old, rattling, broken-down barouche." The countess is deaf and has an ear-trumpet; the marchioness is an honest old termagant, with a voice and temper like a fishwoman's. But this method of treatment insinuates a familiarity, very delightful to the average British reader. It is only another sort of admiration. The change, however, seems to be in the direction of truth, and the English will in time, no doubt, get back to a healthy and common-sense treatment of this subject.

Presumption.

THE East is ignorant of the West, the West is unduly sensitive to the unconsciousness of the East. It is so in this country. St. Louis compares itself with New York, and Kansas City with St. Louis. This succession extends all the way from London to the Sandwich Islands. Before Mr. Bret Harte had won his present fame, I remember to have met a lady from the Pacific who told me that he was the Irving of California. Now, Irving used to be called the Goldsmith of America, and, I suppose, we shall shortly have a Bret Harte of the Sandwich Islands. The indistinct, hazy way in which an eastern community thinks of one to the west of it, is extremely tantalising to the latter. That such a way of thinking of Canada is common in this country may explain in part the hostility of the British Provinces towards ourselves. Until recently most of us thought of the Canadians as a sort of modified Esquimaux. In the same way the English are ignorant and incurious about ourselves. We, on the contrary, are all curiosity and interest in the English. An American has no sooner stepped into the streets of Liverpool, felt the exulting certainty that he is really in the old world, read the signs of the butchers, brewers, and bakers to the Queen, and wondered at the voracity of the great personages of the kingdom, before he begins to ask himself in what way these people differ from, and in what way they resemble his countrymen. This is a matter upon which the English are not at all exercised. That comfortable people, sitting contentedly on their firm anchored isle, are under no pressing necessity of comparing themselves with anybody. The English, certainly, have this advantage, if it be an advantage. The longitude of character and custom is reckoned from Greenwich.

The English very justly charge that Americans

are self-assertive. The American at home is not an especially self-assertive person, or has, at any rate, ceased to be so. But when in Europe our people have nothing to do, and are away from their friends; the people they meet, on the contrary, are in the midst of their native society, and of their life-long employments. It is natural that some defiant or not altogether decorous advances should be made by strangers, who have any quantity of time on their hands. In England, especially, there is some temptation to this, from the manner of many of the people. Some would say, I know, that this is a topic upon which it were best to keep silent. To expostulate with presumption is not the proper way to meet it. Presumption never means to be reasonable, but only to be successful. When you expostulate with an arrogant man you acknowledge the success of his arrogance, which is all he asks. A friend of mine, an Englishman, objected to Mr. Lowell's paper, "On a certain Condescension in Foreigners," that you should never "let them know you see it." Now that is well as a rule for behaviour, but when one is writing, one is supposed to tell the truth. If, as a consequence, the complacency of a man two or three thousand miles away may be increased thereby, why really that is no matter of the author's. How foolish it would have been for Mr. Lowell to have assumed an attitude with which to pique and tantalise an entire empire.

The mere fact that an Englishman is so much nearer the centre of the world makes him seem to himself a better man than an American. This is especially manifest in third-rate men, your "gods of war, lieutenants-colonel to the Earl of Mar." They in some way imagine that their geographical advantage is a personal one. I once sat at dinner near a gentleman of this rank, who had been in correspondence with a very distinguished soldier of the War of the Rebellion. Somebody observed that the General was a good letter-writer. "Oh yes," said the Colonel languidly, "I kept the letters." Here was a little Crimean Colonel, who was actually condescending to preserve the letters of one of the most illustrious living members of his own profession, than whom he plainly thought himself a greater man. I was at a loss to explain it. I believe, though, that the fact that the General lived so far away, and had no famous London or Paris with which to identify himself, was the unconscious cause of this feeling.

English Court Festivities.

AMÉRICANS have an impression that the English think it a considerable distinction to be presented at Court. But the ceremony of presentation has entirely ceased to have any social significance in England. Any young gentleman who imagines that the door of English Society will be thrown open to him on the publication of his appearance at a drawing-room had better save the expense of a dress and carriage and stay at home. If a lady be ambitious of a social success, the money which a robe will cost might be expended to equal advantage anywhere else in London. However, a lady's dress may be worn again, and men may hire a court-suit for the day at a very small cost. Your tailor, if you get a good deal of him, will patch you up something tolerable for very little ; so that sartorial expenses are comparatively light. One can get for the afternoon a two-horse brougham, with a coachman and footman, for a sum less than ten dollars. Still, going to Court costs something, and its only possible advantage is that the spectacle is a fine and an interesting one. One has therefore to consider whether the sight is worth the fee.

A presentation at Court is of quite as little advantage to an Englishman as to a foreigner coming to England. Almost anybody can be presented, and of those who are precluded from presentation, a great many occupy higher positions than many of those who have the privilege of going to Court. Any graduate of a university, any clergyman, any officer in the army, is entitled to go. A merchant, an attorney, even a barrister, cannot ; and yet in England a barrister, or for that matter, a successful merchant, is apt to be a person of more consequence than a curate or a poor soldier. The Court has scarcely any social significance in England. I once asked a young barrister if presentation would help him in the least in making his way in society. He said, "Not a bit."

In England the position of everybody is so well fixed that people cannot well change it by wishing it to be changed. Thus, for a poor East London curate to go to Court would simply make him ridiculous. The parsons in the West-End do present themselves, but there is no part of the British empire where clergymen are of such slight consequence as in the West-End of London. The clergymen, as they file in along with the gaily-accoutred young guardsmen, have a meek and gentle air which makes one feel that they had better have stayed away. No person who is not already in such a position as to need no pushing could becomingly make his appearance at Court. I remember in Shropshire to have heard a family who went down to London to be presented made the target for the ridicule of the whole neighbourhood.

Invitations to the Court festivities are given only to those persons presented in the diplomatic circle. It must be understood that there is at every court in Europe a select and elegant and exclusive entrance, by which the diplomatists come in. Along with them enter also the ministers of state and the household officers of the Crown. The general circle, as it is called, includes everybody else. Another entrance and staircase are provided for it, and in that way all of British society, from a duke to a half-pay captain, gains admittance to the sovereign. When one is in the inside of Buckingham or St. James's Palace the same distinction exists. The room in which the members of the royal family receive the public is occupied during the entire ceremony by the diplomatic circle. Other persons, after bowing to the Queen, pass into an ante-chamber.

Though I say it is of but small social advantage to an Englishman to be presented, yet undoubtedly the greatest people in the empire attend Court, and are to be seen at the ceremonials and festivities at Buckingham and St. James's Palaces. At present the Queen holds drawing-rooms and levees at Buckingham Palace, and the Prince of Wales at St. James's Palace. The latter are attended only by gentlemen, and, though not so grand as the Queen's, are pleasanter. Trousers are allowed, instead of the knee-breeches and stockings which must be worn at all Court ceremonials where there are ladies. At two o'clock—for the Prince is very punctual—the doors of the reception-rooms are thrown open, and the diplomatists begin to file in. First come the ambassadors. It must be remembered that there is a wide difference between an ambassador and an envoy or minister plenipotentiary. The original difference was that the ambassador was supposed, by a sort of transubstantiation, to represent the person of his sovereign. He had a right at any time to demand an audience with the king. An envoy must see the foreign secretary. This, of course, has ceased to have any practical significance in countries which have constitutions; and no doubt a minister can at any time demand an interview of the sovereign. It is still true, however, that an ambassador is accredited to the king, while an envoy is accredited to the foreign secretary. Practically, the difference is that an ambassador represents a bigger country, has better pay, lives in a finer house, and gives more parties and grander dinners. An ambassador has precedence of everybody in the country in which he resides, except the royal family. There are five countries which send ambassadors to England—Russia, France, Germany, Austria, and Turkey. These ambassadors enter the reception-room at the Prince's levee in the order of seniority of residence.

Behind each ambassador come the secretaries of the embassy. After the ambassadors come the ministers. The whole diplomatic corps moves from an ante-room into an apartment in which the Prince of Wales awaits them. The Prince and several of his brothers and cousins stand up in a row. Next to the Prince, on his right, stands Viscount Sidney, the lord chamberlain, who calls off each detachment as it approaches—"the Austrian ambassador," "the Spanish minister," "the United States minister," &c. The Prince shakes hands with the head of the embassy or mission, and bows to the secretaries. When the diplomatists, cabinet ministers, and household officers have all made their bow, it is the turn of British society. The diplomatic circle, and such as have the *entrée* to it, remain in the room: the Englishmen pass out. The Lord Chamberlain in a loud voice calls off the name of each person as he appears, so that each comer is, as it were, labelled and ticketed.

One may often guess the rank or importance of the courtier by the manner of his reception. If he shakes hands with the Prince, you may know he is somebody—if he shakes hands with all five or six of the princes, you may know he is a very great person. But if he gives the princes a wide berth, bows hastily and glances furtively at them, and runs by skittishly, then you may know that he is some half-pay colonel or insignificant civil servant. Something, too, may be inferred from the length of time the Lord Chamberlain takes to decipher the name of the comer on the slip of paper which is handed him. If he scans it long and hard, and holds it a good way from him, and says, "Major Te—e—e—bosh—bow," then in a loud voice, "Major Tebow," you will be safe in thinking that Major Tebow is not one of the greatest of warriors or largest of landed proprietors.

The ceremony lasts an hour and a half or two hours, and during the whole of it the talk and hand-shaking among the diplomatists go on very pleasantly. There is a great deal of *esprit de corps* among them, and perfect equality. Attachés, secretaries, and ministers walk about through the room and exchange greetings. The ambassadors are rather statelier: these do not mix themselves with the crowd of diplomatists, but stand up apart, all five in a row, leaning against the wall.

At all other Court entertainments ladies are present. Of course there are a great many very pretty ones, and their toilets are brilliant. The Queen's levees are very much longer than those of the Prince of Wales. Then, at all ceremonials where there are ladies, men are compelled to wear, as I have said, silk stockings and knee-breeches, shoes, and buckles. One can support this costume in tolerable comfort in a warm room, but in getting from the carriage to the door it is often like walking knee-deep in a tub of cold water. A cold hall or a draught from an open door will give very unpleasant sensations. In many of the large rooms of the palaces huge fireplaces, with great logs of wood, roar behind tall brass fenders. Once in front of one of these, the courtier who isn't a Scotchman feels as if he would never care to go away. Fortunately, most of these ceremonials are in summer, but the first of them come in February, and London is often cool well up into June.

The ceremony of a presentation to the Queen is quite the same as that at a Prince of Wales's levee. The class of royal ladies stand up in a rigid row. On the Queen's right is the Lord Chamberlain, who reads off the names. Next to the Queen, on her left, is the Princess of Wales, then the Queen's daughters and the Princess Mary of Cambridge. Next to them stand the princes, and the whole is a phalanx which stretches entirely across the room. Behind this line, drawn up in battle array, stand three or four ranks of Court ladies.

The act of presentation is very easy and simple. Formerly—indeed, until within a few years—it must have been a very perilous and important feat. The courtier (the term is used inaccurately, there being no noun to describe a person who goes to Court for a single time) was compelled to walk up a long room, and to back, bowing, out of the Queen's presence. For ladies who had trains to manage the ordeal must have been a trying one. Now it has been made quite easy. There is but one point in which a presentation to the Queen differs from that already described at the Prince of Wales's levee. You may turn your back to the Prince, but after bowing to the Queen you step off into the crowd, still facing her. There (if you have had the good luck to be presented in the diplomatic circle) you may stand and watch a most interesting pageant. To the young princes, perhaps, it is not very amusing; but there is plenty in it to occupy and interest the man who sees it for the first or second time. You do not have to ask "Who is this?" and "Who is that?" The Lord Chamberlain announces each person as he or she appears. You hear the most heroic and romantic names in English history as some boy or old woman appears to represent them. One sees a number of beautiful persons. The young slips of girls who come to be presented for the first time, frightened and pale or flushed, one admires and feels a sense of loyalty to.

The name of each person is called out loudly by the Lord Chamberlain. The ladies bow very low, and those to whom the Queen gives her hand to kiss nearly or quite touch their knee to the carpet. No act of homage to the Queen ever seems exaggerated, her behaviour being so modest and the sympathy with her so wide and sincere; but ladies very nearly kneel in shaking hands with any member of the royal family, not only at Court, but elsewhere. It is not so strange-looking, the kneeling to a royal lady, but to see a stately mother or some soft maiden rendering such an act of homage to a young gentleman impresses one unpleasantly. The courtesy of a lady to a prince or princess is something between kneeling and that queer genuflection one meets in the English agricultural districts: the props of the boys and girls seem momentarily to be knocked away, and they suddenly catch themselves in descending. It astonished me, I remember, at a party, to see one patrician young woman shake hands with a not very imposing young prince, and bend her regal knees into this curious and sudden little cramp. I saw her, this adventurous maid, some days afterward in a hansom cab, directing with her imperious parasol the cabby to this and that shop.

This odd jumble of the new and the old struck me again and again wherever I turned.

The mysterious scarlet coaches rolled along Piccadilly side by side with the smart waggons of the Cheshire Cheese and Butter Company. To the traveller who idles away a balmy morning in Green Park, can he resist for a moment the blue hues of the Abbey towers, and the warm shining greensward, this impression is often present. The goblins wont to disport themselves in the mediæval moonshine have been suddenly overtaken by a flood of commonplace daylight. There is the veritable St. James's Palace. But no Charles drives forth from its open portal as in the gay pictures on the curtains of the theatres. The word *belated* expresses the general impression which the monarchical and aristocratic fabric of English society makes upon the observer. It is like the banquet-hall the morning after the banquet; the goblets are overturned, the dishes half-emptied, and the strong sunlight pours in upon the silent chamber, long deserted by the revellers.

The levees and the drawing-rooms may be called the Court ceremonials. There are, besides, the Court festivities, or the balls and concerts at Buckingham Palace. There are four or five of these given in a season—two balls and two concerts. The balls are the larger and less select, but much the more amusing. The ball-room of the palace is a large rectangular apartment. At one end is the orchestra—at the other a raised dais on which the "royalties" sit. On each side, running the length of the hall, are three tiers of benches, which are for ladies and such gentlemen as can get a seat. The tiers on the left of the dais are for diplomatists. English society has the tiers upon the other side. By ten the ball-room is usually filled with people waiting for the appearance of the royalties. The band strikes up, and the line of princes and princesses advances down the long hall leading to the ball-room. The Queen and Prince Albert used formerly to preside at these balls. The Queen does not come now: the Prince and Princess of Wales take her place.

First enters a line of gentlemen bearing long sticks. Behind them come the princesses, bowing on each hand. The Princess of Wales advances first, with a naïve, faltering, hesitating step, a strange and quite delicious blending of timidity and child-like confidence in her manner. Then come, walking by twos, some daughters of the Queen. A German duchess or two follow her. The courtesies of these German princesses are indeed quite wonderful. After entering the hall one of them will espy (such, I suppose, is the fiction) some persons to whom she wishes to bow, and she then proceeds to execute a performance of some minutes' duration. Before courtesying, she stops and looks at the persons to be saluted as a frightened horse examines intently the object which alarms him: she then sinks slowly backwards almost to the ground, and recovers herself with the same slowness. It would seem that such a genuflection must be, of necessity, ridiculous. But it is not so in the least: it is quite successful, and rather pleasing. After the ladies come the Prince of Wales and his suite. The royalties then all go upon the stage, and after music the ball begins.

There are two sets of dancers. The princes and princesses open the ball with the diplomatists and some of the highest nobility on the space just in front of the dais. The rest of the hall is occupied by the other dancers, who later in the evening find their way into the diplomatic set. The dancing in the quadrilles and Lancers is of a rather stately and ceremonious sort. In waltz or galop the English mostly dance the same step, the *deux temps*, and the aim of the dancing couple is to go as much like a spinning-top as possible. They make occasional efforts to introduce puzzling novelties like the *trois temps*, the Boston dip, etc., but, I am glad to say, without any success. The result is, that once having learned to dance in England, you are safe.

The great hall during the waltz is a brilliant spectacle. There are many beautiful women, the toilets are dazzling, and all the men are "flaming in purple and gold." There is every variety of magnificent dress. Officers of a Russian body-guard are gold from head to foot. Hungarians wear purple and fur-trimmed robes of dark crimson of the utmost splendour. The young men of the Guards' Club in gold and scarlet coats, and in spurred boots which reach above their knees, clank through the halls. Scotch lords sit about, and exhibit legs of which they are justly proud. Here, with swinging gait, wanders the Queen's piper, a sort of poet-laureate of the bagpipes, arrayed in plaid, and carrying upon his arm the soft, enchanting instrument to the music of which, no doubt, the Queen herself dances. The music of the orchestra is perfect, and he must be a dull man who does not feel the festivity, the buoyancy, and the elation of the scene.

The dress which our diplomatic representatives are now compelled to wear at the Court ceremonies and festivities needs a word of mention. Our people in America are somewhat conceited, somewhat prone to be confident, upon questions of which they know very little. Congress, at a distance of some thousands of miles from courts, thought itself competent to decide what sort of Court dress an American diplomatist should wear. An able, though crotchety man, brought forward a measure, and, once proposed, it was certain to go through, because to oppose its passage would have been to be aristocratic and un-American. Mr. Sumner's bill required Americans to go in the "ordinary dress of an American citizen." There was no attempt to indicate what that should be. Up to that time our diplomatists had worn the uniform used by the non-military diplomatists of other countries. This consists of a blue-coat with more or less gold upon it, white breeches, silk stockings, sword, and chapeau.

An attempt or two had been made before by the State Department to interfere with the trappings of its servants abroad. Marcy issued a circular requesting American diplomatists to go to Court without uniform. This afforded James Buchanan an opportunity of making one of the best speeches attributed to him. The circular of Mr. Marcy threw consternation into the breasts of certain ancient functionaries of the European courts, for shortly after its appearance the Lord High Chamberlain in waiting, or some other member of the Queen's household, called upon Mr. Buchanan, who was then the United States minister in London, and said that a certain very distinguished person had heard of the recent wish which the American government had expressed with regard to the costume of its agents, and that while she would be happy to see Mr. Buchanan in any dress in which he might choose to present himself, she yet hoped he would so far consult her wishes as to consent to carry a sword. "Tell that very distinguished personage," said Mr. Buchanan, "that not only will I wear a sword, as she requests, but, should occasion require it, will hold myself ready to draw it in her defence." This strikes me as in just that tone of respectful exaggeration and playful acquiescence which a gentleman in this country may very becomingly take toward the whole question. Neither Mr. Buchanan nor anyone else, I believe, heeded the request of the Department, and Mr. Marcy himself, it is said, subsequently repudiated it.

But what was only a request of the State Department in Mr. Marcy's time is now a law. I had good opportunities to know how very uncomfortable the poor American diplomatist is made by this piece of legislation. Its object was, of course, to give him a very unpretending and subdued appearance. The result is, that with the exception of Bengalese nabobs, the son of the Mikado of Japan, and the Khan of Khiva, the American legations are the most noticeable people at any Court ceremony or festivity in Europe. When everybody else is flaming in purple and gold the ordinary diplomatic uniform is exceedingly simple and modest; but the Yankee diplomates are the most scrutinised and conspicuous persons to be seen.

The dress in which our diplomates attend Court at present is a plain dress-coat and vest, with knee-breeches, black silk stockings, shoes, &c. It is difficult to see in what sense this is the "ordinary dress of an American citizen." The dress is not so ugly as it would seem to be; indeed, with the help of a white vest and liberal watch-chain, it might be made quite becoming were it not so excessively conspicuous. An English cabinet minister at a party given in his own house usually wears it, and all persons invited to the Empress Eugénie's private parties came got up in that manner. But in London it was not till recently that American diplomatists were allowed to go to Court even thus attired. Everywhere else in Europe the United States legations were admitted in evening dress, the concession of knee-breeches not having been required. But at

Buckingham Palace no Americans were admitted without the proper garments. The consequence was, that our legation was compelled to stay at home. This state of things continued until Reverdy Johnson came out, who arranged what was called "the Breeches Protocol." Owing to the unreasonable state of the public mind during his term of office, this was the only measure which that good and able man succeeded in accomplishing. The compromise which Mr. Johnson's good-humour and the friendly impulse of the British public toward us at that time wrung from the chamberlains and gold-sticks of St. James's (for you may say what you will, public opinion is irresistible), was to allow the minister and the two secretaries of legation to appear in the breeches above described. Americans who are presented at Court, and who get invitations to the festivities, are all required to wear a Court dress. Of what good compelling the poor diplomatists to make scarecrows of themselves may be I do not know. Mr. Sumner's proposition was just one of those absurdities to which men are liable who have considerable conscience and no sense of humour.

K

Senators and members of Congress fell in with it because they feared to be un-American, and because it is not their wont to be very dignified or (in matters of this sort) very scrupulous.

English Tradition and the English Future.

THE admiration of the novelists of thirty years ago for the British upper class was a symptom of the admiration by the English of that period of everything pertaining to themselves. Each Englishman felt (read, for instance, Ford's "Handbook of Spain") as if he himself had discovered gravitation, written "Childe Harold," conquered Waterloo and Trafalgar, and perished upon the Plains of Abraham. The aristocracy was at the top of British society, and of course great. So that it is difficult, in reading the chronicles of the manners of that day, to distinguish between what is laudation of a class, and what is laudation of the Empire and the period. The novelists can find no words in which to insinuate the immense *immaturity* of anybody who would withhold his applause. Zoroaster and Confucius would smile with wise tolerance upon the cynic and the radical, and would cheerfully assist society by showing themselves at the assemblies. Zanoni, with the personal acquaintance of every interesting individual of the race from Adam down, Bulwer would have thought nothing of until he had entered him at the clubs, introduced him to the party chiefs, and given him enough of the current coin of the realm to astonish the lackeys. That writer describes with excess of definition the Parliamentary leaders. It is necessary that we should be able to recognise to a shade these prime figures in the most important arena of the world. We are not permitted to forget the majesty of these persons even when they are satirised. Readers of "The Caxtons" will remember a letter on colonisation, from the statesman Trevanion to the young Pisistratus. It runs: "Dear Pisistratus: W—— is up! we are in for it for two mortal hours." This letter is dated from the House of Commons, and the Library of the House of Commons! Yet notice the very light way in which the letter leads off. "W—— is up," said in three words, and such short and indifferent ones, too. How fascinating is the disrespectful allusion in the next clause. "We are in it for two mortal hours." W—— is tiresome, no doubt, but can you help admiring the point of view of that man who can make sport of him? The reader must remember the impression made upon him in youth by a description of that most important event, a change of government. There is a most impressive one in Mr. Disraeli's "Coningsby." At three o'clock in the morning, while the boys in the waiting-room of a club in Pall Mall are asleep, a gentleman (I forget his name, but we will call him Mr. Gervase Hastyngs) rushes in breathless and announces that Lord Derby has been to see the Queen, and that Peel has just been sent for to form a government. How striking is the contrast between the commonplace accidents of the scene and the tremendous importance of the moment. One would expect a portent in the sky to announce such an event. There is a new government, and it is only the breathless Gervase

Hastyngs and the hall-boy in buttons who have heard of it. Ah, sleepy Islington, drowsy Clerkenwell, you honest tradesfolk soundly snoring in Clapham, Fulham, Brixton, Hampstead, and Highbury, little you know what goes on among your betters at three o'clock in the morning.

But very little of this arrogance of victory and supremacy remains in England. The tone at present is rather one of diffidence and discontent. There are those who profess to believe that England has lost her ancient courage and her warlike spirit. Now, a nation which has the virtues and the advantages of peace cannot expect to have also the virtues of war, except in a dormant and potential way. To hear the talk of some persons, you would think that war is the state of society for which peace is the preparation, instead of peace being the state of society for which war is the preparation. Courage is a means, and not an end, and it is shown in fighting for the things we want. Englishmen of the present time are not willing to make war for what they do not very much desire. But ought they not to wish to keep their country in its position at the head of the world, which it held fifty years ago? Any such obstinate determination would surely show a great lack of political intelligence. The times change and we change. The new conditions of the Empires of Russia and Germany and the silent influence exerted by this country have altered the face of the world. England does not greatly desire to hold her old place, because she feels that she cannot hold it, and it is only lunatics who refuse to cut their coat according to their cloth. But as to the charge of a want of patriotic feeling and the spirit which takes men well into battle, there can be no truth in it, as any man among the millions who heard the fife and drum play before Sir Garnet Wolseley's returning legions could have known from the beating of his own heart. The tumult of the crowd and the sight of the pathetic ranks of real warriors reveals in the breast of the plainest citizen possibilities of which at average moments he does not dream.

The English now propose to lead the world in a new way. When we go to heaven, we are told, we shall not have fine wines and costly apparel, but we shall not miss them, because we shall have ceased to cherish these carnal desires. The English think—at least that portion of them which Mr. Gladstone represents—that while it is true that they are not hereafter to lead the world after their old fashion, yet that fact should not make them unhappy, for in the new order of things the nations will set little store by mere physical victory. The first duties of a state will be the education of its citizens and the advancement of mankind. The greatest state shall lead the world, not in selfishness, but in unselfishness. That state shall be greatest which is supreme in ideas and in the useful arts. Of course, there can be no disputing the truth of this principle. If the English have a more highly educated population than we, purer domestic life, a more dignified press, a more honourable administration of government and of justice, they are better than we, though we crowd the Continent with our money-getting millions. Gladstone's view is, undoubtedly, the highest, and, undoubtedly, the best, provided always that the state is strong enough to pursue its high purposes in security.

But it seems to me not so improbable that the dream of the English Liberals may have an easy realisation. I know that an American editor in his third or fourth letter home is not unlikely to say something of the palpable decadence of the English power. The observation is often made regretfully, as if the discovery caused him a pang. It is not difficult to understand the state of mind in which these regretful paragraphs are written. His landlady is the only person in the great wilderness who knows him. Nobody marks him. Not a soul in the restaurant or the omnibus recognises him. The main street of the city in which his own paper—the *Chronicle and Evening Advertiser*—is published has no place in the imaginations of the people he meets. He is naturally interested in the points of difference between the newspapers there and at home. But there is in the broad, decorous columns of the *Times*, as they lie open before him in the coffee-room of his inn, an obvious and depressing ignorance of the *Chronicle and Evening Advertiser*. He believes in his heart that the managers of the *Times* never heard of his paper. If the editor of the *Chronicle and Evening Advertiser* is at all a splenetic person, he will shortly have occasion, with mournful impartiality, to suggest the "political decline," the "germ of social disorder," &c. &c.

As for the "germ of social disorder," if the labour question is to be the end of English society, it will be likely to be the end of us also. I am not sure that there is to be a "political decadence." I think that England will find physical security while pursuing the course which her Liberal statesmen have marked out for her in the moral support of the English race the world over. The idea of race is good only up to a certain point. Because a certain number of people in many parts of the earth speak the same tongue (some of them very detestably), it would be very unreasonable that they should join hands against everybody whose patois is different. But so long as England conducts herself with reason, and with that obvious ambition to act justly which now marks her, she will be sure of the sympathy of the Anglo-Saxon race. She will not need support, moral or physical, if she withdraws within herself and limits her purposes by the "streak of silver sea" which separates her from her enemies. But should she feel it her duty to continue her beneficent endeavours for the civilisation of her remote dependencies, she will find that the Pan-Anglican sentiment may do her good service. The silent feeling of the race, even if understood to be but tepidly friendly, will go far to preserve her from extremities. England will be strong in proportion as she has the moral support of the race. As I suppose it to be a mere matter of arithmetic that for the next few hundred years this country will contain the physical mass of the race, I may go farther and say that England will be strong in proportion as she has the moral support of this country. Secure in that support, there is no reason why, with her universities and her highly educated upper class, she should not continue to teach and lead us as she certainly does teach us and lead us at present in almost all the departments of thought and civilisation. Why should not London be the capital of the race?

In such a state of things the diminutive size of England will be a part of her good fortune. Gold is precious because there is so little of it. When the world is full of people who look back to her as the home of their tradition, she will be happy in that her soil will not be capable of dilution. There are leagues upon leagues in America and Australia, but it may be said with pride and affection that there are only a few meadows and a stream or two in England. I suggest this point for the consideration of any American who is to speak at a London public dinner. Let the orator assure his hearers that the race in India, in Africa, in Australia, in America—wherever the Anglo-Saxon pursues his heaven-given prerogative to subdue nature and society—will constitute a mighty moral empire, of which this little island will be the sacred and inviolable home, and he will be certain to sit down amid applause.

Childhood and English Tradition.

A POINT I have not seen made much of is the hold which English tradition and fable and fiction get upon the mind of infancy in this country. When young eyes first open with fresh wonder upon the world, the scenes of English life come in upon us from a hundred sources. Perhaps these impressions are not so strong now as in the days before the war. I see that the school readers now have pictures of the Pacific Railroad with the buffalo scampering from the coming engine. But in my day the pictures in the reading-books were all English; the pictures were English, even if the books were of American composition. The lessons were mainly English, and had to do with English things. It was before the paling of an English cottage that we saw the bent old man, whose age we were told to revere and pity. It was from an English casement that the little girl let the captive robin out of the cage. I was ten before I knew that the lark was not an American bird, and, on being told that I should have a day in the country, remember promising myself that I should hear the bird about which so much was said in McGuffey's "Second Reader." The good boy in that little volume was always rewarded with a tart. Now, I doubt if anybody living in Maryland, Virginia, or thereabouts, had ever eaten a tart, or had seen one to know it by that name. I am sure I never had. But, for that matter, neither had a poet of the last century ever seen an Amaryllis or a Chloë, or heard a shepherd piping in the shade. I must have known that "tart" meant "sour," yet so perverse is the imagination that I conceived it to be a sort of transfigured sugar-plum.

The costume worn by the little boy in the educational work just referred to was quite unique. I fancy it must have been the English fashion of dressing boys of twenty years earlier. The cap was peculiar, though about the year '56 we had something like it called the "Pancake." The collar was a broad band of linen worn outside the jacket. But the portion of his apparel with which I was most profoundly impressed was a pair of incipient swallow tails. The possession of these did not seem to make him any happier, he had become so used to them. They invariably attended him in the orchards, the meadows, the gardens, and wherever his sunlit young existence wandered. Envy of many a childish day-dream, and quite as wise, I think, as some of the more recent ones, how often I pondered them while the cherry-trees stood alone in the silent play-ground, or the echoes of the feet of a solitary passer-by came with a sound of strange and audacious freedom from the pavement of the street below! The little fellow had them on when he and his sister wandered too near the bee-hive. When he looked toward the rising sun, with one hand pointing to the South and the other to the North, it was these little coat-tails he turned to the West.

The household pictures in "McGuffey" all were English, and the groups were certainly presented in an amiable light. How good and virtuous were the families who trimmed the evening lamp in the pages of McGuffey's "Second Reader;" the father, how firm and prudent; the mother, how wise, how tender, how solicitous. (Indeed, the grown people in children's books are always paragons. The readers of the "Rollo Books" will remember that Rollo's father and mother appeared to have been born parents; think of Rollo's father and mother ever being divorced!) There was a picture in "McGuffey" of the little boy I have described walking out at sunrise with his mother to hear the sky-lark. She has told him of dawn and the song of the lark. He has been but seven short years in the world and can remember but four of them; seven years, which in the life of a grown man pass as a week or a month passes. He has never seen the sun rise, but from report and picture he is as familiar with it as if he had witnessed it in Eden. His mother is holding him by the hand, and they are passing a high wall. It is the moist, whispering dawn of a summer's day. Up in one corner of the picture is a little spot which is, of course, the lark, and it is pouring a flood of melody over the scene. The reader may know what that picture must have been to boys whose meadows were the morning-glories which skirted the brick pavement of the kitchen-yard while they waited for their breakfasts, whose butterfly was the winged and dusty grasshopper which tells of August and the close of the city summer!

The sunrise is not often seen by children, except when they are waked early for some picnic or festival. So it is a good theme for the young imagination. The English sunrise has, besides the lark and the milkmaid, all the charming accompaniments of the chase. Whatever confusion there may have been about larks and cuckoos, we all knew that only in the English valleys was heard the horn of the huntsman. There is in the window of a saddler's shop in St. James's Street, near Pall Mall, a coloured engraving of a landscape at sunrise. In the fore ground is to be seen a mounted huntsman amid a pack of hounds. The picture was familiar, for years before I had often come upon it, thrust away in a corner, soiled and torn, in an old garret, where I went in search of lost treasures among handirons and broken hobby-horses. The huntsman's honest plebeian face tells of service for the happy, sleeping people whom his horn will soon summon to the chase. The dawn wakens softly over meadows that have not yet begun to shine. He blows his trumpet, and his jolly cheeks are puffed as he startles the dim dwellings and the drowsy landscape with its saucy echoes.

Now such impressions and recollections as these, existing as they do in many thousands of minds, are of very great importance. They are of real political significance. How ready is an American to greet in England any realisation of these dreams of his childhood! With what pleased recognition does he exclaim, "Oh, this is you!" and "I have heard of you before." I once went upon a visit to a friend of mine, who was an officer in a yeomanry regiment at that time mustering in a town in one of the western shires of England. The colonel, to whom I was introduced, had been a younger son, had gone into the army and been to India. But he had come into his property, and was now a country squire with a large family and handsome fortune. I at once recognised the kind of man. They said he had eleven daughters. (What a fine old English sound they have!) During the mess dinner the regimental band played from a hall adjoining. The colonel, who had put me next him, said, "I wanted to see if the band could play 'Yankee Doodle,' but I find they don't know it." "How good of you!" I exclaimed, deprecating the mention of such a distinction. "Yes, yes," he answered, with the determined manner of one who, though now an old rustic, perhaps, had yet, in his youth, seen something of the world, and knew how things should be done, "I believe in every honour for the diplomatists." As I sat there listening to his honest talk, my mood grew strangely friendly. "Should war's dread blast against them blow," I felt that I wished to be ranged on the side of the kind colonel and his eleven daughters.

The Dancing-School in Tavistock Square.

IN London, in order to "get on," one must be great or famous, or one must dance. Unless a man is a very decided catch and an object to the "mammas," or is enough of a lion to make him fit for exhibition, dancing is about his only utility. The average London man of society thinks dancing a very slow amusement. He is either athletic and prefers hunting and yachting, or he is dissolute, and simple pleasures pall upon his jaded appetite. As a rule, too, the important young men do not dance. The greater a man is, the more is he careful to abstain from anything which will make him entertaining. His dulness is always in proportion to his distinction. The same holds true with regard to conversation or to any other sort of contribution to the amusement of others. He only is agreeable and clever from whom fortune has withheld better gifts than talent or the power of pleasing. He only would be witty who is without solid advantages. A "talking man" is in danger of being snubbed, and nobody can help pitying the ridiculous fellows who sing at the afternoon "musicals."

To be sure, all young people dance. How would "golden youth" be possible if there were no ball-rooms? But when men get toward five-and-twenty, those who can afford not to dance desert the balls for the concert-saloons. Young noblemen and eldest sons will spend a few moments at the parties, and as a great favour to the hostess, will walk through a quadrille with the prettiest girl in the room. But how can one who has at hand the *cancan* and the casinos find amusement in anything so puerile as the waltz? Who cares to talk to humdrum cousins when one may drink bad champagne with painted women in a gilt café near the Haymarket? It is only cadets, clerks in the Treasury, youths with no particular expectations, who dance. Among diplomatists, attachés waltz:

a councillor or secretary may under protest. I knew one excessively light-headed envoy who would dance now and then, but who always took care to dance badly.

The talk of the young men concerning balls and parties is, however, to be taken with some caution. They are "bores," and this tone the poorer young men catch from the more fortunate swells. A clerk in one of the offices, when I asked him his destination, said, "To this —— ball." Of course, the young man would have been very sorry not to have got a card, but he shuffled off to "this —— ball" with the air of a martyr. Dancing young men, however, are scarce enough to make ladies who give parties anxious to get them ; and if one is going to a ball, though it may be more dignified to walk about *solus* and stare, it is certainly pleasanter to dance.

Accordingly, when a diplomatic appointment made me a resident of London, I determined to learn to dance. Cato learned Greek when he was eighty, and I was twenty-five before I could do the *deux temps.* I was reared in a pious household, in which dancing was thought to be wicked. After leaving college I acquired a notion of my own dignity quite inconsistent with so frivolous a pastime. (I give my experience in this matter at some length, because I know it will represent that of a great many others.) But, of course, I outgrew this dignity in time, and came to look upon that notion as only another and rather small sort of coxcombry. Between your frivolous and your philosophic coxcomb I much prefer the former, as the more amiable of the two. What possible relation had the conduct of my legs to the universe and the moral law? My fear of dancing was a symptom of that timidity and strength-destroying self-consciousness which possesses so many people of the present day. They are enamoured of superiority, and they associate certain external images with the fashionable types of greatness they admire. A little energetic thinking would easily rid the victim of such reverie. What this philosophic coxcomb really fears is not the essential unworthiness of the pastime, but the impression of himself he reflects in the minds of lookers-on.

Omne ignotum pro mirifico, says the proverb. I should have been taught to dance in order to learn that dancing is no very wonderful thing. A man who could put his arm round the waist of a pretty woman, and calmly trust himself with the guidance of his floating argosy of lace and tarlatan about a ball-room, was formerly to me like a being from another sphere. I could not understand how that man felt. His *ego* was an exalted mystery. A few steps at Brooke's academy would have taught me that this man was but mortal, and might have cured me of my depressing sense of inferiority.

I once did attend the dancing-school of a little village in Western New York. This village was the seat of a very radical water-cure, in the chapel of which there was a service on Sundays and a dance on Tuesday evenings. The ladies were all in Bloomer costume, and as the institution was radical socially as well as in religion and politics, the cooks, laundresses, and chambermaids were always asked to the balls. These were, in fact, the only healthy people present. Your vis-à-vis was usually a lady with an affection of the neck or a gentleman with a wet towel round his forehead. One gentleman, I remember, with a towel about his head and a neck awry, had a chair set for him which he occupied while the side couples were dancing: when the time came he sprang up with great alacrity, gallantly and playfully flung out his right foot, and walked through the step in the most punctilious manner.

One's imagination was not fascinated by the felicity of whirling round the room one of these invalids in short clothes and trousers. Still, I did go to the village dancing-school with the intention of learning to waltz. But I found it was only the little girls who were pupils: their sisters merely came to look on and chat. I did not care to enact the directions of the master before all the smiling young society of Bunbury. The only pupil of riper age I ever saw at the school was Miss Carker, the lady doctress from the water-cure. She was dressed at the time almost like a man, and her hair was parted on the side. She presented herself as a scholar, and the professor, who had never seen her before, was sorely puzzled where to put her. He did not like to ask her. There was a long continuous row of children standing at the time, the upper half of which were girls and the lower half boys. The professor wittily extricated himself by placing her just in the middle and letting her decide for herself.

In London I found it quite necessary that I should put myself under the care of some instructor, and I was commended to the academy of Mrs. Watson, in Tavistock Square. Tavistock Square, the reader will remember, is situate in the dim regions of Bloomsbury, once an aristocratic quarter, but now quite given up to lodging-houses and the private dwellings of attorneys and merchants. Here lives on the second floor an economical widow, who supports a son at the university; a Spanish conspirator, Communist, or exile of the Thiers government occupies the third; an American Senator, even, who is verdant or unambitious, may find his way with his family into the first. Upon the whole, it is a gloomy neighbourhood. All Bloomsbury has much the same look—the most unlovely part of London, or indeed of England. For my part, I believe I prefer Seven Dials.

Mrs. Watson was a very large woman. She was, however, a very good and agreeable person, and an excellent teacher. There were besides several nieces, rather pretty girls, who assisted her in the education of the young men. It seemed to me an odd sort of profession for a young lady. Twelve hours out of the day and twelve months out of the year they were saying, "Take my right hand with your left, and put your right arm ——" This latter instruction the preceptress did not finish in words, but the pupil seemed to comprehend his duty by intuition. "That is very well," said the lady.

These young ladies were very nice, and of course perfectly respectable, but they did not appear to me to be envied. Society is not kind to a poor girl in England. That her position here is different is due not to any superior charity or chivalry of ours, but to our luckier circumstances. Society in Europe assumes toward her that tone of scarcely concealed contempt which the strong and successful must inevitably hold towards the weak. The talk of the young men concerning her is, I think, not so respectful as in this country. Of course, where such a sentiment exists, the dignity of the objects of it must be somewhat impaired. It is only the exceptional people who can resolutely hold their own sense of themselves against the mood of society.

These ladies, I say, assisted Mrs. Watson. She herself usually undertook the initiation of the patient. Mrs. Watson was not only large, but strong, resolute, and conscientious. Moreover, she was not a person to put up with any indolence or false shame on the part of a pupil. I had for years been enamoured of passivity. "I do not like to be moved," says Clough. That poet and much-musing philosopher liked to feel himself at the centre of innumerable radii of possibilities, rather than as moving in any one line by which he was plainly and irrevocably committed. But Mrs. Watson was not a person to encourage any indecision of this kind. After a preliminary word or two she took me firmly by each hand and began jumping me back and forth, saying, "One, two, three, four," &c. Be it remembered that I was the only performer in the room, and that all the lady assistants and a pupil or two, who were waiting their turns, were looking on. Mrs. Watson, becoming satisfied with my proficiency in the piston movement, wished to see what I could do in a rotary way. She began by sending me round the room by myself, spinning like a top. When I gave signs of running down, she struck me again on the arm and sent me round faster. Really, for a person with some pretensions of sobriety, this was pretty thorough treatment. I was sure the young assistants must be screaming with laughter, and I was not sorry when I passed into the hands of these milder and less muscular preceptresses.

I was very proud when I had learned the *deux temps*. I really thought myself a very accomplished young man. But Mrs. Watson said that it was quite necessary, absolutely indispensable, that I should learn the *trois temps*. I had got on very well with the *deux temps*, but what labours I underwent in the acquisition of the *trois temps*, and what giggling of the lady assistants I braved, and what screams of stifled laughter from a very jolly cousin of Mrs. Watson, who was visiting from the country, and who came in to look at us, I will not here relate. I was absolutely made to stand on one foot and hop. It was incredibly painful, but I bore it all, as children take medicine, because I thought it was good for me. The reader will fancy the bitterness of my feelings when I discovered that it was all in vain. The *trois temps* was not danced at all in London: the *deux temps* was universal.

There was no personage of the dancing-academy in Tavistock so interesting to me as its mistress, Mrs. Watson, whose gentle and dapper little husband played the violin. Mrs. Watson was rarely seen except on great and critical occasions. Her full habit of body and long service entitled her, she thought, to repose. But she would now and then walk with majesty and old-time elegance through a figure of a quadrille, taking hold of her petticoat with thumb and finger of each hand, and coquettishly fanning and flirting it. She did not often waltz or galop, but sometimes, in enforcing a lesson, she would commit herself to the undulations of the dance, and sail or swim about the room, *sola.* She was as a rule a very good, kind, and sensible woman, and she had, moreover, a few fine antique graces which she would bring out when circumstances seemed to call for them. Among these was a very superb method of leaving the room which she gave us occasionally. If the conversation turned upon fine society (I believe she thought me rather a man of fashion), and if she had seen my name in the *Morning Post* that morning, she would treat me to one of these. "I bid you good morning," she would say; and lifting her petticoat with thumb and finger, she executed a retreat backward with some six steps, and, laying her hand upon the door-knob, vanished with a peculiar grace and dignity.

Of the school in Tavistock Square, besides the accomplishments which I there gained, and which I highly prize, I retain a little memento in the shape of Mrs. Watson's "Manual for Dancing," a tiny book which now lies on my table. It contains, besides descriptions of quadrilles, polkas, galops, &c., much excellent advice upon general behaviour which recalls the little institution quite vividly. Occasionally the little document becomes severe, almost sarcastic. "All skipping, hopping, and violent motion should be restrained." Again we are told that vis-à-vis must not meet each other "with proud looks and averted glances," but "with a smile" and "a pleasant recognition." "True politeness is entirely compatible with a kind disposition. In our higher classes unreserved and agreeable manners prevail much more than in the middling ranks of society."

Contrasts of Scenery.

I HAVE never been so struck with the sublimity of great cities as in August eventides in the depths of dog-days. At such an hour, when in London, I used to go to Trafalgar Square. Instead of the usual paltry plots of grass, that square has a broad floor of stone, which immensely enhances its impressiveness.* Only a few weary feet broke the stillness of the place. The golden clouds of dust choked the vistas of the streets. Silently out of their grimy mouths the fountains glided. I heard all round the desolate roar of the city. The granite column seemed borne upward and to swim in the

* There is a profuse and profound wealth of fancy and expression in this line of one of the sonnets of Shakespere,—

"Than unswept stone besmeared with sluttish time."

air, and Nelson from its summit looked far away to Egypt and the Nile.

Art is stronger than nature in the old countries. Nowhere in England do you ever get well out of London; the town inflames the island to its extremities. London is strong as disease is strong. Many a time, swinging about the streets in the "gondola of London," the hansom cab, I have wondered that so great a place should be so *low*—should have so little height. The inequalities on the surface of an orange, we are told, vastly exaggerate the hills and valleys of the globe. London is scarcely higher than if the surface of the earth upon which it lies had been scratched with a file. Yet so potent has it been to change the entire face of that part of the world which it dominates.

Nature has been chased out of England into the sea. In Europe man is scarcely conscious of the presence of nature. Here nature is scarcely conscious of the presence of man. Perhaps, indeed, on our Atlantic border, she is just waking to a sense that her rest is broken by the foot of the intruder. But in England nature has been quite subjugated.

The fence and the furrow are everywhere. You find yourself by a lonely tarn at the bottom of a sweet breathing ravine, and you say, "Surely here is something primeval;" but you have only to look up to where the sharp back of the mountain cuts the sky, to see a stone fence riding it with a giddy tenacity, and holding on for dear life. We miss the feelings with which newer and wilder scenes inspire us. English scenery is always pleasing, perhaps the most agreeable for any common condition of mind that can be found. Nowhere is there such a pretty country to have picnics in. What wind so careless as that which fans the cheeks of August tourists, whose table is spread half-way up some hill-side in Devon? In the morning, when the youth of the day supplements the age of nature, then we see the English landscape in its best. The air is sweet and the sod greener than elsewhere, and the foldings of the hills and hollows are lovely and surprising. But the beauty is for the eye; it fails to touch the heart. This seemed to be true even of the scenery in Wales. It was very impressive. The Welsh mountains were very old; the wind of the heather wandered gravely from the sweet, sad fields of the most distant part; the verdure of the margin of that shining estuary that sets up to Dolgelly, through the greenest green, is enriched by the yellow of the buttercups.

Nevertheless there was an incompleteness that I could not suppose to be altogether in myself, for the ocean had its moods as sublime or bright as where its evening waves flow round the light-ship at Sandy Hook. The waters came to the cottage thresholds and to the gates of the gardens. Late one afternoon, as I sat looking over the blue, bright ocean, there came under my window a proud-stepping fellow with a plaid, and a feather in his bonnet, playing upon the bagpipes. A pure and stainless sunset was approaching. The sweet breeze from the heather ran about the streets at will. Far out over the quiet, flickering waters wandered the notes of the bagpipes, flew, and were wafted westward. The children danced about the piper, and their feet moved to the music and to the fast-changing moments of the sunset. But the landlord came out before the door bare-headed and rang the bell, and the bagpiper ceased suddenly and went away with the children, and the sun dropped down behind the wave, and I, with that rude haste with which we extinguish delights we know to be too evanescent—went to dinner.

For the purposes of comfort the English climate is better than ours. I have heard this denied, but am sure that it is so. One has only to remember that the fashionable hour for horseback riding in London is from twelve to two in the summer months. Nobody can ride at that hour anywhere in this country. The equestrian here has a choice between sunrise, sunset, and moonlight; unless, as used to be common in the South, he rides with an umbrella. But for poetry and the observance of nature our climate is better. The English summer never commits itself. It is always lingering April or premature October. If you go out at night to walk in the moonlight or to sit by the sea-shore, you must take an overcoat. Here, about the last of June, we have a sweltering week or two, in which everybody unlearns the use of overcoats. We then understand that it is summer, and that it will stay summer. To be sure, if you are in search of some poor churlish spot where you may forego nature and the miracle of summer for the sake of keeping cool, you may find it on the coast of Maine. But if deeper pastimes entice you, and more verdurous hill-sides; if you would sit in some rose-embowered porch, while yet the blue-eyed mist lingers in the farthest recesses of the mountain gorge, then it is to the Susquehanna or the Kanawha you must go. There, where the chestnut shade cools the edge of the hot, humming meadow, you may lie, your hands stained with the dark, deep clover. On indolent afternoons your scow will float through those silent scenes, you hearing only the dull lapping of the river at the thirsty keel.

I may here say that one great disadvantage for any person desiring to look at an English landscape is the absence of good fences to sit upon; the ground is usually too damp to permit one to lie full length. I missed very much the rail fences of my own country. I would come to a pretty prospect, and my legs sinking under me, I would look about for a place to sit. The inhospitable landscape had not a single suggestion. There were no stones, and a hedge was, of course, not to be thought of. How different the stake-and-rider fences of this land of ours! The top rail of a good fence is as fine a seat as one can wish. Of course, much depends upon the shape and position of the rail. Sometimes the upper rail is sharp and knotted. But one has only to walk on for a rod or two before a perfect seat can be found, and this point I have discovered to be the very best from which the scene may be viewed. It really appears as if the honest farmer had builded better than he knew. If there is one place from which to overlook a landscape to be preferred to another, I have always found that nature, so far from betraying him that loved her. had actually put there the properly shaped rail at his disposal.

The streams of England are unclean. Waters that the poets have made famous smell abominably. Consider the task the poets would have to immortalise all the running water of our Atlantic slope. Unsung, unnamed even, with pure noises they hasten to their river-beds. For many miles by the railway which traverses North Wales, the Dee brawls along with a tumult of green waters. From the car window it looked enticing, and I thought I would stay over a day at Llangollen and walk along the banks. At Llangollen is "The Hand," over which presides a gentle and unique landlady, who carries a bunch of keys, and greets you with that curious cramp of the knees called a courtesy. (If you would see a courtesy, you must go to England very soon, for the Radicals will have put a stop to it in a year or two more.) There was hanging in the coffee-room a picture of Sir William Somebody, the great man of the neighbourhood. His left arm he rested upon the withers of a great black hunter, while his wife, buxom and beautiful, leaned upon the other. Some happy dogs were playing about his feet. There were two or three more engravings of the kind well known to frequenters of English inns. Upon a table in the middle of the room were the cold meats, the pies, the tarts, the custards, and the berries. In the corner, a lunch was spread for two collegians who were travelling with their tutor. All this you saw to the music of the old blind harper, who sat just outside the door by the high clock in the windy hall. Here, too, was the prettiest girl I saw in Wales. She told me she was sixteen, and I believed her. You talk of strawberries and cream—a namby-pamby and silly expression—she was blackberries and cream. She was there with her brother Arthur, a youth two years older than herself, the guide, philosopher, and financier of the party: the pair were the children of a Bristol music-teacher. We lunched together, and the girl cut the pie with her own hands. She had been twice to London. When I asked her where she stayed when she came there, she said, "At Mr. Hawkins's," as if that were enough. Was there ever such a delightful answer!

I tell this because it is only fair to Llangollen that I should. Any little nameless stream in the Shenandoah Valley is better than the Dee. But in the tavern near there would have been no landlady with the keys, nor the really good music of the harper, nor the table spread with tarts and berries, nor very likely the pretty girl. The green waters of the Dee, cool and clean enough a few rods off, I found, when I came nearer, washing over noisome, stinking rocks. I followed the slipping banks a mile or so, and then took the macadamised road that runs above the river. I very soon found my way back to the inn, and went with Arthur and his sister to a village entertainment. We sat upon the front bench, and saw a burlesque of the Field of the Cloth of Gold, performed by four metropolitan stars, upon a stage eight feet by twelve.

I have spoken of art as strong and of nature as weak in the Old World. In scenes in which art and nature mingle, England, I suppose, is unsurpassed. The little I saw of rural England was mainly on Sundays, and then I could rarely get far away from London. There are influences which nature appears to borrow from society. The Christian Sunday seems to impart to the pristine beauty of our own landscape an intenser purity. Here, where the virgin altars are set up in glades whose stillness is broken only by the noise of the primeval streams, where the spires shine afar over our summer wildernesses, the face of nature is conscious of the religion of man. There is, on a Sunday afternoon, in the long street which climbs the hill of a New England village, an unattainable severity, an almost bitter silence. On a Sunday morning, when the village bells are silent, to me, sitting under the trees of an orchard in blossom, there is in the air a strange reproof, a pungent purity, which renders obvious a canker in the midst of the blue sunlight and the bloom. These impressions must of course exist in England, though my occupations in London were such as to give me little leisure to taste the wild silences and asperities of the rural Sunday afternoon. In one of the few suburbs of London yet comparatively free from the ravages of convenience and respectability, there was an old green-walled garden-plot, to which I was permitted to repair at that hour. I sat alone upon a broken, dirty, iron bench (I beg the T——'s pardon for calling their bench dirty), and under an old pear-tree. It was a long patch of sod and flowers. The brick walls were rent and decayed, and, except where the peach and the vine covered them, were green with moss and black with age. The neighbouring gardens I only knew by the tops of the pear and may-trees. No sound came from them save the rustle of their greenery, which now and then disturbed the heart of the quiet hour. Of the children who played in them, of the maidens who knelt among their flowers, I knew nothing. The same sunshine and yellow haze filled them all, the same Sabbath silence. From out their narrow plots all looked upward to the same blue sky. I used to think that the gardens never ended, but lay side by side the island through, and that the sea washed them all around.

New York and London Winters.

AN English winter all men have agreed to consider as the greatest discomfort under which the inhabitants of the Isles suffer. The day is dark by two, and one can scarcely read before ten in the morning. Yet the densest, yellowest fogs in which poor Londoners grope from house to house to find their door-bells, the all-day rains that drown the cabbies, and shadow the large, dark, hospitable windows of the inns—all these are very pleasant, soothing, and inviting in comparison with such persistent slush and foul weather, such protracted out-of-door misery as we suffer sometimes in New York. There is a jerking and incessant quality in our winter weather. It is no sooner allayed and softened than it is up and at it again, until patience can support it no longer, and one yields one's self to be jolted along by fate. An English winter is disagreeable rather than violent; it is no such tax upon human nerves and patience as our own. Of course, your feet are never clean; your eyes smart with the fogs; the east wind withers you; but you are, somehow, soon beset with a soft and dirty uncomfortableness, to which, once having succumbed, you continue in contented subjection.

We are not sure that the overhead London winter has not been a little slandered. The sun comes out at times very softly, and as you look over the wet sod and blue wintry thickets of Green and St. James's Parks, the towers of the Abbey catch from the air a natural or artificial blue, exquisite and quite indefinable. But they have nothing like the exhilaration of our cold moonlight and starlight heavens. They have nothing like our successive days of hard, bright weather. They have nothing like that frozen blue-green sky of our January nights, with the moon apparently congealed in the midst of it. On a late Sunday, looking over the bay at sundown, there arose a scene so wild, strong, and sublime, that the beholder could scarcely believe himself in the midst of a city of a million people. The desolate bay, jammed with ice from the wharves to the wood-fringed Jersey hills, lay as silent and stern as any untrodden unfamiliar place in the heart of the Andes or the Himalayas. There is a vital hour of the landscape, which, at summer sunsets, is very evanescent. The day concentrates into its parting glance a swift, intense meaning. Turn your back upon it a moment, or shut your eyes, and it is gone; but, on this evening, all around the city roofs, the hills, and the ice-fields, there lingered a deep, strong crimson almost frozen into the sky.

The puissance of nature over man here, and its unconsciousness of him, even in the very ways of his cities, is strangely apparent to the European. We shoot about the rivers in our ferry-boats, and wheel in our omnibuses through the drifts of the streets, and all the time the snow-storms roar over us, and the whirlwinds enwrap us and hide us from skies which scarcely notice us, and shut us in from a world upon which we scarcely make any impression.

The Evening Call.

THE evening call is a peculiarity of American life. The strict watch kept over the family would make that institution, as it exists among us, quite an impossibility on the continent of Europe. In England, where there is greater freedom for unmarried women, this evening cannot very well be used for calling, owing to the lateness of the dinner hour. The question of dinner is, indeed, very much involved in the matter. It is quite impossible that it should be later than six without either unhappily shortening that ceremony or infringing on the hour for the call. While dinner is certainly a pleasanter meal taken in the evening than earlier, we must remember that the evening is the best hour of the day for social enjoyment, no matter how we pass it. It is the instinct of man to have the best thing last; we should always be happiest just before going to bed. Yet in considering the question whether the evening is better as we pass it, or as the English do after an eight o'clock dinner, there is much to be said on both sides. Both ways are undoubtedly good, but upon the whole a change to the English custom would be rather for the worse. Comparing roughly the *pros* and *cons* of the subject, we might say that the English habit is better for families, and our own better for the morals and well-being of the bachelors.

We would certainly not underrate the magical effect of a dress coat and white bosom upon the drooping faculties. The English dinner makes a rubicon dividing by a broad line the day of work from the day of relaxation. The diner washes off the toil of the day with its soot and grime. No matter how tired or languid he may be, the mere act of dressing seems to put a new song in his mouth. He becomes pert and audacious, and bears down upon his acquaintance with the delight and pharisaic feeling of cleanliness and good apparel. He has a distinct consciousness of his linen. He is well aware of the difference between himself and any unclean thing. All this is very pleasant. The English dinner certainly has this consideration in its favour, and for families even higher ones.

But it bears hardly upon the bachelors, who transact their solitary meals with speed, and have nobody to go to see. On the score of comfort, though, some bachelors in England are very well off. The club men, as a rule, need no sympathy; their misfortunes are not of the material kind. The miserable people are the men who are compelled to live at the hotels and restaurants. The British lion who stares out of the club windows is a well-kept contented beast. But there is no happiness for that lean creature who, as hunger possesses him, must lash his sides with his tail, and wretchedly reflect whether he will lie in wait at the nearest chop-house for whatever comes along, or daintily devour a bird or two at the Pall Mall Restaurant, or pounce upon a leg of mutton at Simpson's in the Strand. The club is the admirable result of long experience. Not in vain have the bachelors of the past lived and suffered. Pretty furniture, good cooking, and agreeable company unite to make a pleasant impression. The dining-rooms, which are usually small, have perhaps a dozen tables, one of which the diner has to himself. A wax candle is placed upon each, with a white paper shade about it. The cloths and napkins are spotless, and the glasses glistening. Men usually read at dinner, when alone, books or magazines out of the library; and two men who have not much talk, even when dining together, will read. The young men usually dress; and the room, with its pretty tables, and its florid, well-dressed occupants, makes an agreeable, appetising impression. Physically, then, the bachelors are well enough off. In other respects they are not so fortunate. Their privations begin when dinner is over. They must then go to the smoking-room, and have coffee and chat; or, pleasantly gorged and fuddled, lounge and bask before an open fire. This, again, is not so bad, but they tire of it in time. The trouble is that one half of the great human race is excluded; they wish to see that other half, and there is no place where they can find it. Ladies' society is very difficult to be had, because families are at their pleasant and leisurely dinners. There may be, here and there, people you may run in upon; but the universal opening of doors, which takes place from eight to nine in American towns, is quite unknown. The British bachelor, therefore, as he rises from his dinner at the club, is an object of commiseration. What is he to do till bed-time? He may have a rubber of whist in the card-room, but that is expensive. He may go to the theatre, but the play is not always good; and, if it were, he does not want the play every night, any more than waffles every morning. If he has force and restlessness, he is driven to all sorts of shifts to amuse himself. I knew one young gentleman whose post-prandial diversion it was to rush off to ride to fires on a steam-engine, and blow the trumpet. But for men gifted with less energy than this individual possessed, the last resort (sometimes we fear the first) is the society of the ladies who frequent the Argyll and the Alhambra. Many of those gentlemen, very likely, do not feel their privations. Most men about town in London might think the way of spending the evening in vogue among us exceedingly slow. But the vitiated taste is the result of the evil experience. Had they possessed our opportunities from youth they might have thought differently.

But those fortunate people, whom fate has not compelled to toil, are comparatively rare with us. After a hard day's work, it must be a very energetic man who cares to ride to fires on an engine and blow the trumpet; and for men who labour in the daytime, no conceivable relaxation, as a stand-by or staple, could be better than the evening call. It is fortunate that this very good thing, unlike most other good things, is easy to be had. Almost any young man, coming as a stranger into an American community, may at once secure the society of good and kind women. Of course, in any city, and almost in any village, there are people whom the young stranger will find it difficult to know. But there are plenty whom he may know easily, and who are quite as good. There will always be some who think they have friends enough, and there will be others who hold notions of chaperonage and surveillance, but the tide of democracy makes very little of these things.

The young man will find friends somewhere to his mind, and such friends will usually be feminine, the indispensable quality men ask in their acquaintance. We say then that the stranger will find women who will like him, and they will be better than he deserves to know; for in this country women are very equal in education; the difference in mental and social culture between classes is mainly seen in the men. It appals Europeans to hear of the readiness with which strangers are received into American homes. But before we censure our way of doing, we have to consider two points. Is it good for the young men, and is it bad for the families into which they are admitted? The advantage to any friendless young stranger is indisputable. A merchant in St. Louis has told me how, when a boy, he left his New Jersey home for the western town, which was then a week's journey off. The very evening of the day on which he reached St. Louis, by good luck he found his way to a parlour where there were an old piano and some young ladies, and these young ladies sang him "'Way down upon the Swanee River." The lad was but seventeen when, to seek his home and future, he stepped down into the cold current of that dreary stream. He says that the song, and the kindness of the girls, warmed his chilled breast as with a cordial. We do not think that families have very much to fear from a very liberal opening of doors to strangers. There are dangers in our society, but things would not be helped by a more rigorous examination of candidates for admission. The probability is that if you do not like the candidate he will not like you, and will take himself off before he can do you any harm. It is quite as safe to trust a countenance as the word of an introducer, though it is well to have both. The introducer is liable to mistake. Moreover, you have no security that the boy who grows up in the next garden to your own may not turn out a knave. We cannot but regret any movement that tends to narrow the possibilities of intercourse. Unluckily, it is our doom to know too few of the admirable people who exist.

Society, as seen in the parlour of an American house by the evening caller, is the social unit or *plenum*—small enough to permit him to be a part of it if he chooses, and so large that he may treat it as a spectacle without being accused of staring. It suits everybody, from the plainest youth with the common gregarious instinct to the more conceited person who looks on and admires. I believe this simple institution is one of the best possible tests of the moral health of any epoch of one's life. There are two such gauges. If our minds are not open to nature, if it bores us to sit upon a fence and look over a darkling country for an hour after sunset (providing, of course, we have ever liked that sort of thing), we may think that something is the matter. This is a negative way of getting at the truth. But in the presence of the pure and beautiful our decadence is shown us plainly and unequivocally. Take the parlour of some household where goodness and refinement are the family dower, and the voices of shame and strife come from the outside muffled through its windows and walls. The mother is there, and she may remain if she choses. The abolition of chaperonage has robbed her of her terrors. If she has kindness, or authority, or benignity, or any other beauty, we consider her an acquisition. A father or brother is not in the way. Then the daughters and sisters, or the cousins who are visiting, sing, or crochet, or talk, or sit silent—it makes little difference which; for, if they have grace and innocence, we defy them to move an arm, or thread a needle, or walk the length of the room, without expressing it. There, in the deep and tranquil scene before us, we see written those stories of truth and purity that happily we may so often read in the broad pages of the book of human life. In such hours elevation and sensibility come of course. How grateful we are for whatever virtue we possess, how glad of past self-denial! But if the late months contain an ugly recollection, how darkly it smites us that the truth cannot be told in this fair company.

Our Latest Notions of Republics.

THERE is something to me indescribably moving in the attitude of sympathy, yet of separation, which this country held towards Europe for the first third of the present century. That continent was so far away we scarcely believed it to exist; yet in our remote happiness and security we were unable for an hour to avert our eyes from the drama of human fate enacted within its cities and upon its plains. We later Americans can scarcely understand the wonder and attention with which the citizens of our earlier republic looked upon Europe. When the young ladies of that period gathered to tea-parties in my own native village, it was under the very shadow of the stone tower of the church where were said the longest prayers in all Virginia, that they thumbed albums containing pictures of Haidee and the Maid of Athens; and who was it but Byron, the libertine and sceptic, that they held in their dear little Presbyterian hearts? My mother, in that mountain home, sang of the loves of Josephine and Napoleon, or thrummed upon the old piano to the humming-bird in the honeysuckle vine, the "Downfall of Paris." Thus did our early republic, nestling along the edge of the great unknown continent, hear the echoes of Europe. Each wind that swept the sun-washed sea brought tidings from the land of passion, and feud, and discord, and ambition. Armies met and perished. Patriots languished in prisons and expired upon scaffolds. But no blight reached those happy homes, only pity and enthusiasm. No rumour stirred for an hour the trance of our summer landscape. The mountains yet stood silent; the spires lingered in the virgin air; still the wave of the ocean lapped the long glistening line of sand that rimmed our Atlantic border.

Our early attitude towards Europe was one of separation. We admired Europe far more than we do at present, yet at the same time we were much farther away than now. We looked on with wonder and sympathy, and yet all the while prayed to be delivered from temptation. Unable to take away our eyes, we crossed ourselves. Mirabeau wrote a pamphlet in which he warned us that in the Cincinnati Society (which association, I believe, continues annually to eat a dinner somewhere) we held the germ of an aristocracy; and Virginia, with the charming simplicity of the time, refused to retain a chapter for this very reason. If you had told a patriot of that day that his dream of a republic would be one easy enough of accomplishment, that in fact it would be no such great thing when attained, that kings and lords were the simplest and most easily mastered of the obstacles in the way of human progress, that a state of society in which the humblest citizen could be elected to office might be a very immature one, you would have nearly broken his heart.

The passion for the spread of political liberty, so familiar to all cultivated and generous minds during the first half of the present century, has diminished very noticeably of late. Hardly a vestige remains of that enthusiastic sympathy which the people of that day gave to Greece and Poland. It is but twenty years since Kossuth, it is but ten since Garibaldi and the impulse of Italian unity. So that only in the last decade of years has the change of which we speak come over society. In Europe the phenomenon may be in part explained by the great interest the common people have taken in social questions. But in this country there has been much less interest in social questions, and we must look for some other explanation of our apathy toward the spread of republicanism abroad, and of our want of enthusiasm and exultation over its indisputable establishment at home. I think that the decline of our aspiration for the spread and establishment of republicanism is the result, first, of the sense of the fulfilment of that aspiration, and, secondly, of the fact that we had greatly over-estimated both the difficulty and the importance of the task. America, with whose movements Europe has always so strongly sympathised, has had several kinds of patriots. The patriot of the years following our revolution was of a far more ardent and interesting type than his successor of the present day. His task was almost as new as that of Columbus. The world applauded, and admired, but doubted, and it would have been strange had he not felt the contagion of its disbelief. He believed, but believed with fear and trembling. He was full of forebodings and warnings as to the fate of our liberties, had the lessons of Greece and Rome continually on his lips, and attached a superstitious value to Washington's dying utterances. The early patriot adored liberty, but with the ardour of the lover for his almost unattainable mistress. The patriot of the present has taken her, not for his sweetheart, but for his comely and contented bride. Comfortably he sits in dressing-gown and slippers, and, without surprise or exultation, sees her who was once his morning star tripping about his apartment, hanging ornaments on the bare walls, dusting away the cobwebs, and putting to rights on doorstep and window-sill some disorderly things which have long been a scandal and a reproach in the eyes of certain aristocratic old maids over the other way. Indeed, one might say that the patriot of the present finds his vocation a dull one. With human ingratitude and obliviousness, he hardly understands that he is a very happy man. If you tell him he is fortunate in his freedom from royalty and hereditary aristocracy, he is rather surprised. It is much as if the Swiss should congratulate him on not having the goitre. Really that is one of the things it had never occurred to him to be thankful for. The American patriot of ten or fifteen years ago was also a person of more vigour and enthusiasm than the man of to-day. Politics is with us a far less ardent and attractive field now than then. It lacks, at present, the inspiration of opposition to slavery. We all felt before the war (those of us who dared dream of such an event) that the abolition of slavery would make the country happy and perfect. And during the war, how looked then, in the future, the vine and fig-tree under which the victors should one day cool themselves! How we heard the distant church bells ringing, and saw far away the piping times of peace, and the wide, brooding land grown happier for ever.

It has all come to pass. Our dreams have been more than fulfilled. We are rich and free, and wield a silent influence such as perhaps no other country wields. But we have attained to this only to find ourselves much duller, and no nearer perfection than before, and to again confront tasks of Herculean difficulty. In our pursuit of principles which are new and true, we had forgotten some that are old and equally true. We now call to mind that no State can be happy in which there are not wise and good men to direct and teach, and in which other men are not willing to learn. We have entire confidence in our republican success, and we know that, great as our difficulties are, kings and lords cannot help us. It will come right in the end, we are sure, with higher and wider education, and that recognised supremacy of an educated class which we once had, but which we threw away. But our task is so grave that we have little time or inclination for sympathy with the impatience of other countries.

English Conservative Temper.

THE English Conservatives have rather a temper than a policy. In describing a Conservative, therefore, it is far more important to observe him than to attempt a diagnosis of his opinions. He is the balky horse of the team. And yet he is the balky horse in front of a car that must go on. Rear and plunge as he may, he must get ahead, or the single-trees will be upon his heels. The hard pulling has always been done by the Liberal horse, the Tory steed trotting on sullenly by his side. As soon as the Liberal animal stumbles or shows signs of fatigue, the balky horse at once begins to plunge in the most indignant and contemptuous manner, and to indicate to the charioteer that if the coach is to proceed that stupid beast must be unhitched. The Tory steed (which has really considerable mettle and energy), finding himself the sole reliance of the vehicle, strains forward with all the strength he can command. But the poor beast is nearly exhausted with the struggle before the car has been got over a few feet of ground. The Liberal horse must be again called in ; sullenly the unhappy beast resumes his reluctant jog. But we must not despise the Conservative horse. He has his uses. He is a good war horse. When the car of state becomes an artilleryman's carriage, he rattles it over the stones in fine style. To change the figure somewhat, he is no beast to carry on his back a tax-gatherer or an educational reformer, or social philosopher who turns his toes out. But when a soldier gets astride of him he becomes a serviceable animal.

The Conservative party in England has always been the party of objection and the party of defeat. It has its important uses. It teaches caution to those whom too much success would render over confident. The flippancy, the jaunting, joking tone of men who think it scarcely worth while that they should condescend to be serious—that tone into which the successful majority in our own civil struggle fell after the war was over—an English party is rarely allowed to reach. The evil to which men are prone as the sparks fly upward is much too inevitable a matter to permit the Conservative function to become an obsolete one. It guards a wise and good impulse from the old age of Solomon. The Conservative party has, moreover, accidental allies in the caprice of the people, in all sorts of rumours and humours. There was evident in the recent crisis an irritable, wilful disposition for change, as if the people were tired of looking at Gladstone. They were like untutored listeners at a concert of classical music; they enjoyed none of it, but when the orchestra was playing they wished it was time for the singing, and when the prima donna was at her solo they wanted the fiddles to begin again. But the Conservative party must always be beaten. The idea of reform has taken a permanent hold of the English mind. All parties agree that progress is the principle of government. The rankest Tory in England holds that freedom should broaden slowly down from precedent to precedent. He only sticks at the particular reform. Reform is a good thing: but he thinks that you must not increase the suffrage, and you must not have the ballot, and you must not disestablish the Irish church. In a word, the Conservative party must always have a policy at war with the necessary and inevitable principle in the life of the state.

English and American Newspaper-writing.

THE decorum which is characteristic of English papers of the best class resides not so much in the men who conduct them as in the audience to which they are addressed. Were not such decorum required from the outside, persons without education and breeding would be sure, sooner or later, to begin to write in papers; indeed, educated and well-bred men would soon cease to write without decorum. It must be a man of uncommon virtue and strength of judgment, who will write in accordance with the principles of good sense and good taste, unless those principles are pretty well defined by society. What may and what may not be said are pretty well understood by writers in England. The feeling of the limits put upon them checks many a low impulse, dilutes the gall dripping from many a pen; while the consciousness of a critical audience represses the gush, folly, and pretence which impose upon the ignorant. The best papers of England are read by tradesmen, and perhaps by mechanics. But it is not the tradesmen and mechanics who compel the papers to take their sensible and decorous tone. The barristers, the clergy, and the educated men in general of England do this, and the merchants and mechanics acquiesce. The English have a larger class than we of men who ask of any proposition or measure if it be true or right, rather than if it be useful. Here, one is more apt to belong to a clique, or to have an axe to grind, or to have interests other than those of opinion in the matter. Interested criticism, indeed, is that heard everywhere most commonly; but it is still true that the number of men who care for truth and justice, simply as truth and justice, is smaller here than in England. An educated Englishman, in expressing his opinion upon a question which concerns his country and another country, will usually profess to exclude the consideration that England is his country. I say "profess;" of course, he will not always—perhaps, not often—do it, but an American will scarcely profess to ignore his interest in the matter. This is largely because higher education is more diffused in England than here. Then it is true that education necessitates a certain degree of honesty. Even if the conscience of an educated and able man does not make him truthful, the clearness of his perceptions will often render it difficult for him to be false. One evening, sitting in the gallery of the House of Commons, I heard a striking example of that candour in which educated men delight. An opponent of the Government was upon the floor. He was upbraiding the ministry for selling arms just before the outbreak of the Franco-Prussian war, at which event, he averred, nobody was or could have been surprised. This was a roundabout way of intimating that he was not surprised, and that he was a person of some foresight. Mr. Lowe rose, and before proceeding to the matter of the speech, dismissed the orator as follows: "Mr. Speaker, the only criticism I have to make upon the gentleman is, that he expects everybody to be as clever as himself. Because he descried in the future the terrible war that has ravaged Europe, saw Metz, saw Sedan, the capitulation of the emperor, the fall of Paris, the Commune, and all the rest of it, he thinks that I should have seen all this too. Now, in all humility, I assure him that I never expected anything of the sort. Mr. Speaker, the whole thing has been a complete surprise to me." The wit and truth of this were irresistible.

Of course, there is wonderfully little stuff in the usual editorial page of the usual high-class English paper. For that matter, it is inevitable that there shall be very little stuff in the editorial page of almost any paper. The writing about this country is very poor: it is not, as a usual thing, hostile or spiteful; it is rather feeble and inaccurate. The best writers, those most ambitious really to comprehend the country, shoot wide of the mark. In one way they have studied us pretty well. They have read the "Federalist," Madison's papers, &c., and have quite a notion of State's rights and the Monroe doctrine. But of the moods of the country and its physiognomy, of our public opinion and its factors, they know little, and, as a rule, write ill. A man born and reared here, and accustomed to think about his country, will detect constant little divergencies from the truth. The pen of the writer is incessantly glancing from reality, by spaces which it would be difficult to define, and yet of which it is impossible not to be conscious. Sometimes we are treated to columns of pure guessing. But the mass of English writing about America we should describe rather as the "wishy-washy complimentary." The chief editor of a journal says, "America is a great country, and she must have to-day a portion of our space." Accordingly, some young gentleman is selected to maunder down a column of loose, uncertain comment, which is not to offend the Americans, who are touchy, nor to tell the truth of them, of which last article they are in possession of very little.

But when we turn to our own papers, we find the editorial articles feebler than the English ones; while the propriety, scholar-like manner, and semblance of fairness of the English press are generally wanting. And here I have an opportunity to speak of the affectation and insincerity so common in American editorial writing.

An editorial should be written to inform the people concerning some question of the day, or to counsel the public as to the course to be pursued concerning it. A newspaper writer should speak as if he were in a deliberative assembly, and the question under discussion were to be voted upon. How often does he so speak? Read through the usual editorial, and ask yourself, "Now what shall I do?" You find that you are as much in the dark as ever. Suppose the Modoc war is to be written upon. The gentleman or lady sits down to the task, talks in a most superior manner, and earns his or her ten, twenty, or thirty dollars a column, whatever it may be, to the entire satisfaction of the managers of the paper. But now take the article to the Government authorities, and let them educe a policy from it. The public functionary must read a long time before he will discern whether or no he is to hang Captain Jack; whether, indeed, he is to do or to refrain from doing anything in particular.

It is the faith of many newspapers that the

people do not like sense and information; that they prefer nonsense or commonplace which has the appearance of originality. Now I think that the "average man" is very well contented with either. He likes sense and information, if they are not put in such a way as to tire or shock him. He is willing enough to put up with commonplace which imitates originality, for he finds nothing to object to in the commonplaces, and he has not sufficient confidence in his own judgment to detect the counterfeit originality. But it is a mistake to imagine that there is always a popular demand for any foolish fashion of writing which happens to exist. That very lack of discrimination which marks the uneducated man renders him quite as ready to accept sense as nonsense. But as nonsense only is given him, he accepts nonsense. Who is he that he should set up his opinion against persons who express themselves in such fine and confident words, whose sentences are printed in such elegant type, in papers sold at such grand hotels, and scattered by the thousand in such great cities? What is known as a popular demand might be more accurately described as a popular acquiescence. It seems very formidable when we think of the immense number of persons who form it; but then it is only skin deep. Instead of a popular state of mind being, as we are apt to think it, a recondite and almost inscrutable matter, it is oftener the result of an obvious and even contemptible cause. Instead of there being a deep-seated and characteristic taste with which public caterers must comply, the fashion is often given the people from above. After the fashion is fixed, men write in accordance with it, and explain its existence by the fiction of a demand. The qualities at which editorial writers may aim are sense, thoroughness, and good taste. Now and then they may be eloquent, and now and then they may be witty. But wit and eloquence must be the incidents, and not the staple, of an editor's work. If we try to have it otherwise, at the best we can only have sham wit and sham eloquence, which are not only false, hurtful to the writer and hurtful to the reader, but must be quite as tiresome as honest commonplaces.

It is natural that an editor should be more

anxious that his labour appear good than be good. He has special temptations to this sort of work. He is paid less for the inherent than for the apparent value of his contributions. A lawyer's work is good when he wins his case, a doctor's when he cures his patient; but there is no such test for the work of an editor. "Do people like to read it?" is the ultimate question; and what people like to read cannot easily be known with certainty. As we are confident, however, that sense and thoroughness must be acknowledged, we marvel that writers are not more willing to rely upon honest work and to be content with it. But that is the last thing they are willing to rely upon. They must have an out-of-the-way title. They must torture the jaded humour into some feverish antics. They must put their trust in affected wisdom and affected fine moral sentiments. One peculiarity of their way of writing is a certain tone of infinite knowingness. A fact is told you, but it is parenthetically insinuated that the writer's general knowledge of the subject is simply boundless. Is he to write upon the Eastern question, and has he heard for the first time of General Ignatieff, he begins as follows: "Well, in spite of the wily Russian who represents the Czar in Constantinople," &c. Very few of the English papers, except the vulgarest, exhibit this peculiar form of nonsense in their treatment of questions of politics; but the best papers occasionally do something very like it in their criticisms of art and literature. The imitators of these critics in this country are, however, quite even with them. A friend of mine, who is an editor, sent me a book of poems to review, with the request that I should make the article "dignified." I knew very well what he meant by this prescription. I was to talk as if I were not only familiar with the subject in hand, but with pretty much every other. I was to be very confident; here and there derisive, here and there ecstatic, but always absolute; and each paragraph, as I left it, was to stand up and quiver with a gelatinous consistency, galvanised by the energy of my mind and hand.

One would naturally wish to speak only when one can speak strongly, and with precision and certainty. The seemly man is he who is silent when his thought is immature. He is not likely to offend his own self-esteem, nor to lower himself in the opinion of the clear-sighted. But the seemly silent man and the unseemly speaker are alike immature. We merely see the one state of mind, while we do not see the other. One confesses the mental condition, which the other equally possesses. So long as the speaker does not lay claim to a certainty which he has not, he is really as good a man, and, if not so seemly, as dignified as the other. It is one's duty at times to write ill. A newspaper contributor must constantly write upon subjects of which his knowledge is imperfect, and of which his opinion is immature. It cannot be otherwise. And why should writers wish to make it appear otherwise? You consult a paper with the same intent with which you ask the opinion of an intelligent friend. You do not wish your wiser friend to decide the matter for you; you ask him to throw light upon it. If he has no definite opinion to give you, you wish the stimulus of a common sympathy and a common curiosity. You ask the same of a newspaper. The writer need not be omniscient; if he be eager and interested the reader will be eager and interested. The disposition in newspapers to appear wiser than they are is therefore not only immoral, but, I believe, inexpedient.

Americans Abroad.

MANY sorts of Americans are to be seen in Europe. There are those who live there and have a hold upon society. These are the privileged few; and some of them are very nice people and do us credit. But even these are not quite so nice and certainly not so useful and considerable as if they lived at home. For a foreigner is always at a disadvantage. He is tied to the country in which he is resident neither by his past nor by his future, and is therefore not important to it. Even an eminent foreigner cannot hold abroad the place he has at home. He has done something in his own country, and is of some value there; he will be apt to be of very little value elsewhere. So that it is certainly true that a man loses in social density by having his residence in a land other than his own. Men who desire achievement and consideration should live at home. No country, not even our own, is hospitable to foreigners as such; our ladies are glad enough to have a count at their houses, but I never hear that they put themselves to much trouble to seek out young strangers who are over here making their way.

But there are certain other Americans (and this class is much larger than the foregoing) who count upon their fingers the grafs and princes they know. They are very unhappy people. Their unhappiness does not consist in the illusive and unsatisfactory nature of the phantoms they pursue so much as in the agonising self-inquiry of which they are the subjects. They never cease to interrogate themselves with one form of ancient question, "What am I?" They ask not "Am I virtuous?" "Am I right?" but "Am I genteel?" "Do I possess that peculiar constitution of mind which, in the illustrious circles of the Old World, makes me 'one of them?'" This question is never answered. If it were only a tangible society the inquirer was in search of, his condition would not be so wretched; he is condemned, however, to imitate the pursuit of the dog who ran round after his own tail. Alas, if men could but devote to the pursuit of goodness and knowledge the sensitiveness of conscience, the earnestness, the profound desire and dissatisfaction with which they ask to be genteel!

Some thirty years ago the English were the great travellers of Europe. They overran the Continent. Many of these tourists were of a sort to make Frenchmen and Italians wonder what manner of men the English were. But the fact of such people getting abroad was altogether to the advantage of the English. Persons of corresponding position on the Continent would never have got beyond their own thresholds. Of late years, however, the Americans send abroad more travellers and spend more money in foreign lands than any other people. Wealth having in this country, far more than in England, lost significance, any sort of people here go abroad. It is greatly to the credit, or, at least, to the advantage of this country, that such people can prosper and be happy. It is true, however, that we have very often cause to be ashamed of our brethren in

Europe. Why is it that Americans look so much worse abroad than at home? The truth is, I suppose, that we see a worse class than we see at home, or see more of them, and that we see them under circumstances which are not in their favour.

As I have before said, any foreigner is seen at a disadvantage in a country not his own. He is especially at a disadvantage, if he lacks social education. He is amid circumstances to which he is not accustomed, and if there is any vulgarity in him it is sure to come out. Indeed, if he have none, he is likely to adopt a little for present use. A civilised instinct is possibly the cause of some of his mistakes. He is alone, would like acquaintance, and is not judicious in his advances. There are some things which the wariest traveller will have to learn. One is that it will not do to be candid; an Englishman, Frenchman, or German quite as much objects to be told anything ill of his country as an American. A foreigner should admire; even guarded and discriminating praise from him is not usually acceptable. I believe that one other mistake with which an American goes abroad for the first time is, that because he lives in an important country he is entitled to more respect than men who live in smaller countries like Holland or Belgium. A little thought should teach him that this cannot be; that one's nationality must be, of course, a very small ingredient among the considerations that go to make up his presentibility. Is he good-looking, is he rich, well-mannered, amusing, learned, clever? These are the questions which society asks, and not, "What is his country?" But an American's chief danger in Europe is that his energy and want of occupation may hurry him into improprieties and vulgarities. I know it is true that Americans who have lived long about the European capitals, and who have nothing to do, are not energetic people. There are many of our countrymen, loiterers in the foreign cities, who have learned to suffer in silence the *ennui* and stupefaction which idleness generates. Never having learned the pleasure of labour, and fancying that they cannot work as other men do, they give themselves up to an unhealthful indolence, of which they do not admit to themselves even the wretchedness. I have seen a man kept out of Paris by circumstances he could not control, varying the monotony of existence in the following manner: One day he has his chop at Simpson's in the Strand, and his supper at the Pall Mall Restaurant; the next he has lunch at the Rainbow (calling for porter which he does not like, but which he understands should be had at the Rainbow); in the evening he dines at the Blue Post and has whitebait. So he goes on from day to day, exhausting one by one the experiences of the universe.

But the usual American abroad is not this sort of man, and has temptations of a different kind. The more he is able to rest the better for him. One danger is that his impatience and activity will carry him into scenes livelier than the above, but not so moral. Especially he should beware of too great a desire to know the world and to "study society." Every reader is familiar with that strong feeling of obligation resting upon him to acquaint himself with certain French novels ("an educated man should know these things") before he has read much more famous works of a less peculiar character. In the same way it is surprising to find what opportunities for the student of man the casinos and other places of the kind seem to afford. It is not unusual to see at the Argyll, just when the dancing is the wildest, and the dull electricity in the atmosphere the most palpable, the really honest traveller from America—a Sunday-school teacher, likely—"surveying mankind from China to Peru," &c., and looking on with a countenance expressive of edification and enlightenment. I had here better amend a remark made above. I spoke of the innocent and dull delights of certain feeble idlers. I meant to pass no encomiums upon the morality of American idlers in Europe. The tendency of the sort of life led by these persons, especially when unmarried, is to produce a certain type of man of which one sees a great deal—a sort of cross between a *roué* and an old maid.

It is certainly true that our people do not look to such advantage abroad as at home. I presume the reason of that is, in part, that here we form intimate acquaintanceships with people whom we like, and these stand for America to our minds and "wall us out" from the inferior sort we meet abroad. What a delight it is for the sojourner in a foreign land to meet a really charming American family, with beauty, sense, refinement, and kindness! These people are happy to see the fine things Europe has to show them, and will be happy, likewise, to go back to the land which their absence has made lonely. I have no words to offer such as these. But other good persons, with minds less firm and hearts less refined, may reflect with advantage to themselves concerning the manners and the state of mind with which to travel.

Society in New York and Fiction.

I HAVE heard young persons who contemplate writing an American novel, or who are interested in the literature of this country, speak of the material there is in New York society for the writer of fiction. It seems to be thought that certain people living among us may be made to have, as members of society, an interest separate from that we feel in them as men and women. A great many good and amusing books have been written about London and Paris society; why may not such books be written about New York society? Now I wish to show that there is no society in New York which corresponds to that of London or Paris, and that any writer who attempts to make the idea that there is the key-note of his work will be likely to produce a silly, vulgar book. Apart from the harm to the writer of such a misconception, it is not well to be putting into the heads of people, the country through, notions which have no actual truth. And be it observed that I am now discussing only a question of fact. Whether or no there should be such societies, or whether, where they exist, they do good or harm, I do not say. I only say that there is no such society among us, and that novelists should not write as if there were. But the fact is not of literary importance only; if it be a fact, it should be recognised and accepted by the country.

It would be difficult to discuss this subject without some reference to democracy, the triumph of which in this country has been so complete. There are yet some unreasonable discriminations concerning employments among us, but it is certain that the movement of public sentiment has been strongly and rapidly towards democracy. There was, during the early years of our existence, an approach to a national aristocratic society in this country. A governor or a senator, a judge, commodore, or a general, was an aristocrat. Anybody who represented or reflected the dignity of government was an aristocrat. This feeling continued till near the middle of the century, or until the second generation of statesmen had disappeared. It has gone now "where the woodbine twineth," to use the significant expression of the significant Jim Fisk. The extreme weakness of the aristocratic element among us at present is in part—in very small part—to be explained by the want of respect in our people. A plain man in this country cares nothing for the man who is above him; is rather proud, and believes it to be a virtue, that he does not care. Nor does it appear a thing to be regretted that such a state of mind exists in the humbler citizen towards the greater one. It is well to have A admire B, if B is a person of superior rectitude, energy, and intelligence. But what advantage will it be to society to have A admire B because B lives in a better house, and may have a better dinner than A?

There is no need to put the cart before the horse. The value of veneration among the masses of men is obvious where they have anything to venerate. And there can be no want of the capacity for respect among our people. Some story now and then is told which discloses the vast reverence in which Hamilton and Jefferson, and later, Clay and Webster, were held by the Americans of their time. "Break up the great Whig party," said Webster on one occasion, "and where am I to go?" I remember to have heard my father, who was an old-line Whig and an adherent of Webster, say that Webster admired Isaiah. The impression made upon me at the time was very distinct. I thought how conceited the prophet would be were he only aware of the great man's eccentric partiality.

A writer has spoken of this country as one in which superiorities are neither coveted nor respected. That is not true; real superiorities are certainly respected. The few that we have are, perhaps, respected too much. Americans having acquired the just idea that Mr. Emerson is a great man, proceed to let him do their thinking for them. The bulk of our reading people know enough to recognise what is excellent, but have not the critical self-confidence which is the property of educated men. They therefore fail to insist upon the fact that the greatest men have their limitations and cannot include everything, but in a kind of dazed reverie, like that of a patient in typhoid, accept whatever is told them. So it is not true that there is a want of respect among people in this country to those who deserve respect: the contrary is the fact.

The national aristocratic society has disappeared with the disappearance of respect for the politician. What is called "position" is in this country now altogether local. This is necessarily true. A is known among his neighbours as a rich and decent person; his wife and daughters are "nice" (the American for "noble"), either absolutely or relatively to the people about them. A has position, therefore, in his own town; if he moves elsewhere he does not inevitably take it with him. Now, in very little and very simple communities, these ideas of position and precedence are not important. In a very great place, on the other hand, few men are large enough to be seen over the whole town. As a consequence, we see that New York is perhaps the most democratic town in the country.

It has become so during the years in which it has been shooting into a position of such national and cosmopolitan importance. It is now quite as democratic a place as the inevitable varieties of accident and talent among men will permit it to be. The artifice of exclusiveness, which is sure to succeed in a smaller place, will not do here. People greatly desire to do what they find difficult to do. They do not care at all to do what they know they may do. Accordingly, in a town, or city of moderate size, the people who wish to be thought better than their neighbours, and who have some little advantages to start with, are wise to keep to themselves. They thus prevent their neighbours from finding out that the excluded and the exclusives are just alike. They have for their ally that profound want of confidence of ordinary people in their own perceptions. But this is a device which will not do in a city of the size and wide-reaching importance of New York. What will some mover of commerce or politics over the face of the country care for the opinion of the gentlewoman round the corner, who thinks him vulgar?

Thus we see it to be impossible that any dominant society may exist in this country. The recognition of this fact should teach quiet to people inclined to be restless. It need not be unwelcome to the friend of man, for he will remember that democracy does not mean the triumph of utility over dignity and refinement, but that it means dignity and refinement for the many. Writers of fiction may regret the want of diversity and picturesqueness which the fact involves, but it is always well to know the truth; if they desire to avoid vulgarity and the waste of such opportunities as they have, they must heed it. To make men and women interesting as members of society is denied them; but should these writers have the wit to paint men and women as they are, the field is wide enough. There are on all sides people who are charming to contemplate, and whom it should be a pleasure to describe.

THE END.

www.ingramcontent.com/pod-product-compliance
Lightning Source LLC
LaVergne TN
LVHW050522100826
845148LV00002B/420

9781425520717